THE LAST TABOO

THE LAST TABOO

Saying No to Motherhood

ROSEMARY AGONITO

Algora Publishing
New York

Library of Congress Cataloging-in-Publication Data —

Agonito, Rosemary.
    The last taboo : saying no to motherhood / Rosemary Agonito.
       pages. cm
    Includes bibliographical references and index.
    ISBN 978-1-62894-087-9 (soft cover : alk. paper) — ISBN 978-1-62894-088-
6 (hard cover : alk. paper) — ISBN 978-1-62894-089-3 (ebook) 1. Motherhood.
2. Childfree choice. I. Title.
    HQ759.A337 2014
    306.874'3—dc23
                        2014025352

Printed in the United States

TABLE OF CONTENTS

INTRODUCTION

I confess my guilt. Much of what I urge others not to do in this book, I did. I did it because I was unthinking about the single most important thing any human being can do. I did it because my education, despite purporting to teach me to think, never pointed me to the really important questions that go the heart of human life as we live it day to day. I did it because there was no voice urging me not to. On the contrary, every voice I heard said, "Do it." The messages, explicit and implicit in the culture, shouted, "Have babies."

Imposing life on a human being is the most serious and awesome responsibility any of us will ever take on. Yet most of us do it without thought because it's *the* thing to do, especially for women. Having children — a family — is what just about everyone wants (or thinks they want). "Family" conjures up warm feelings of caring, love, respect and mutual support. Some sort of family is the ultimate home we all seek — the resting place, the haven in hard times, the escape from the world.

But a "family" does not require children. It can take many forms. A family can be two adults, one adult and a child, two adults and any number of children, an extended family of blood relatives, a group of unrelated adults who make a home together, or any configuration of adults, with or without children. We can have a family and a haven without children.

Yet the "need" to have children persists. Long after the sexual act stopped requiring pregnancy thanks to birth control, the cultural and religious imperative remains: propagate the species. Despite all their hard-won advances, women in the modern era are still expected to have babies.

A number of assumptions underlie the ongoing baby boom. Generally, we believe that (1) each person has an absolute right to have children, (2) breeding (perpetuating the species) is an obligation each person has, and (3) existence is always better than nonexistence. Each assumption stifles debate and reflection on the most important and most personal question of all.

The first assumption is perhaps the most deadly. We produce babies on the unthinking assumption that we have an absolute right to do so. Circumstances — personal, familial, social, global — count for little or nothing in the face of this perceived right. We are aghast at the Chinese policy that limits the number of children a family can have. After all, the Chinese have the same right everyone is presumed to have — the right to bear children at will, unlimited by any circumstance, including mass starvation. Folks of all political persuasions, conservative to liberal, assume this unfettered right.

Not only do we believe in the absolute right to have children, the second assumption goes further, assuming we have an obligation to produce offspring. In practice, that obligation falls squarely on women who bear children and typically rear them. The obligation may be seen as religious or social. Religious dogma imposes motherhood on women as the central obligation of her life — fulfilling her divine mission of making souls for the Almighty. Socially, we assume an obligation to perpetuate the species and insure the survival of humanity. Religious or social, the mandate is "Be fruitful and multiply."

Finally, we cling to the unspoken assumption that to be is always better than not to be. It is the same impulse behind the drive to stop every suicide, including assisted suicides of the terminally ill, regardless of their suffering or the absence of any human level of existence. It's the belief of "pro-life" folks, who demand that existence — life — be imposed on every fetus regardless of the horrors or pain that existence promises.

So, rich or poor, married or single, educated or uneducated, depraved or moral, we think everyone has a right to have children and to have as many as they want. We think it's better for every child to exist than not to exist, regardless of circumstances. And most think that at some point, a woman *ought* to have a child. Whatever else a woman may accomplish in her life, the thinking goes, it amounts to little or nothing next to motherhood. Indeed, historically, womanhood has been equated with motherhood.

We are wrong on all points. There is no absolute right to have children. There is no obligation to have children. And surely, nonexistence can be better than existence, practically and morally, in many circumstances.

The right to bear a child is a qualified right, not an absolute right. Anything we do that is potentially harmful or destructive on many levels cannot be viewed as something we have an absolute right to do. In the wrong circumstances, motherhood can impose a horrible life of mental and physical suffering or deprivation on a child, undermine the well-being of mother, father, and family, and harm society and a fragile environment with finite resources. There are minimal standards that define a human life, minimal needs that qualify a life as human. Unlike many animals, a child is utterly dependent on an adult's ability to provide not only food, clothing, shelter and security for an extended period, but also companionship, love, nurture, and education. Put simply, anyone who cannot provide for the physical well-being of a child and offer love, caring, emotional and moral support, or who is putting that child in harm's way, has no right to bear a child.

The notion that every woman is obligated to have children is as absurd as the idea that everyone has a right to have children. *A biological capacity to have children, in itself, hardly qualifies or obliges anyone, female or male, to be a parent.* Addiction, temperament, a penchant for violence, an inability to nurture and love, lack of financial means, age, and prolonged absence present only a few of the impediments to fulfilling the requirements of proper parenthood. But even with the best parents, there are many circumstances so terrible that willfully bringing a child into those circumstances may be considered immoral. Yet parenthood — the most difficult and important job in the world — requires no qualifications, tests, or experience, unlike virtually every other occupation. Instead, every birth is congratulated.

Of course, the obligation to reproduce and nurture children falls in practice on women whose lives will be forever changed by motherhood and, with rare exception, limited by it. Women need to explore those changes and limits fully so they are not victims of a cultural mandate masked in images of cooing babies in soft blankets surrounded by a halo of joy.

Because motherhood is the ultimate serious act, it can best be justified when it results from careful thought and deep love and caring for the child-to-be, oneself, the family, the community and the environment. This grants, of course, that a woman has an option — and many women in undeveloped countries and religiously repressive cultures do not.

Motherhood should not follow automatically from a cultural mandate dating to a time when breeding was necessary to sustain an agricultural or nomadic existence and infant mortality was high. That world no longer exists for most people. Today, the arguments against becoming a mother are at least as important as the reasons for becoming one, yet those arguments remain strangely silent.

A new life will enter a world full of great beauty and profound ugliness, soaring achievements and horrible degradation, wealth and poverty, love and hatred, health and disease, power and powerlessness, joy and suffering, plenty and famine, peace and war. All without any say in whether it wants life or not. Even in the best circumstances, life can be hard.

Beyond the child's and mother's lives are the global issues. With the world reeling under overpopulation and an environment whose resources sputter in a state of terminal destruction, indiscriminate breeding by humans can no longer be justified. The world is radically different today than it was five hundred — or even one hundred — years ago and requires a different mind-set. The traditional approach to motherhood isn't working anymore.

The old question, "How many children should I have?" must give way to the more fundamental question, "Should I have children?" A reflective examination of reasons for and against motherhood is needed. *This book is not a prohibition against mother-*

hood, but seeks to help women say "no" to motherhood when the circumstances are not right, when her needs or her preferences or her family's well-being do not align with the overwhelming cultural mandate to have babies.

Looking only at the negative — why and when not to have a child — rather than exploring the pros and cons of bearing children may seem one-sided. *The book does not explore the reasons why a woman should have a child because those reasons are everywhere.* From the time a little girl is born and is given her first doll, she will breathe air that drones endlessly, "Your mission in life is to be a mother." She will hear a zillion reasons why she should have babies, why she will not be "fulfilled" if she does not, why she will not be a "real woman" if she fails to bear children.

Yes, the approach is one-sided — deliberately so. I will not point out the joys of hearing a child's first words, or the thrill of seeing a child's face on Christmas morning, or the wonder of watching a child grow and discover the world. These are real and wonderful. I experienced them with my children. *But it is not my goal to tell you what you already know.* If any message has been presented in a one-sided manner, it is the one that tells us that children are the center and joy of life. Volumes have been written on the joys of motherhood.

The pretty face of motherhood is everywhere. I have focused on the not-so-pretty face of motherhood.

I pose an alternative for women who believe, consciously or nonconsciously, that they *must* have children. I seek to help women with the most difficult decision of their lives, to trigger a debate about motherhood where, for too long, the glorification of motherhood has stifled dissenting voices. It's important for someone to speak the unspeakable.

Finally, do I ignore fathers? After all, isn't fatherhood as serious as motherhood? Isn't it as important for men to be able to say "no" to fatherhood? Yes and yes. But in the final analysis, it is women who control the processes surrounding the birth of a child — conception (except for rape, incest and living in a culture or religion that strips women of any choice), birth control, abortion, bearing the child, getting adequate health care for the fetus, bringing the child to term. It is women who will experience physical trauma for nine months and during the actual birth. It is women who nurse children, women who still have the primary physical and psychological burden of rearing the child for many long years. It is women whose lives are dramatically altered by having a child, women who are expected to constantly service the needs of their children, women who make the career accommodations, women who are blamed for the child's failures. When men nurture children, they are the exception and they do so despite male culture and upbringing.

This book in no way diminishes the responsibility and role of father or the fact that his life is changed by the presence of a child or that he, too, must make accommodations to that child. But that is the subject of another book and I welcome someone else writing it.

CHAPTER 1. HELP! I'M TIRED ALL THE TIME

The Physical and Emotional Impact of Having Children

Mommy in the Supermarket

As he sat in the supermarket cart, the small boy whined, "Mommy, I want this," while he grabbed a large Snickers bar from the shelf and trust it in her face. Mom, who had momentarily averted her attention to a little girl clinging to her skirt, turned and said sharply, "Put it back, Billy. It's almost dinner time." I pushed my carriage past the trio as Billy began to wail at the lost Snicker bar. We met again in the next aisle. Billy still whimpered as mom wiped his running nose with one hand and reached to put a box of Captain Crunch in the carriage with her other hand. The little girl had started to tug in earnest at her mother's skirt.

"Mommy, I want to go home. I'm tired."

"I'm tired, too, sweetie, but we have to finish shopping."

I passed them again at least three times and each time mom was dealing with some new crisis or complaint. Billy grabbed a bottle of jelly from the shelf as his mother reached for the honey. I had walked a few steps past them when the crash of breaking glass drowned out the voice on the loudspeaker hawking the special of the day. Shards of glass and purple jelly littered the floor. Chagrined, mom ordered Billy and sweetie to stay put. Walking carefully on her high heel shoes and looking very out of place in her dress-for-success suit, she gingerly stepped around the mess to hail a clerk stocking shelves.

That crisis past, mom succeeded at one point in engaging Billy and sweetie in the shopping enterprise. She handed the goods to each in turn so they could toss the item in the cart. But soon, "My turn!" was followed by "No, it's your brother's turn," followed by sweetie whimpering, "Billy did two. It's my turn!"

In the next aisle, Billy had to go to the bathroom — real bad — now — no, he couldn't wait till they got home. Off she went, literally dragging sweetie as she hurriedly pushed Billy toward the restroom. The look of disgust and sheer exhaustion on her face made me sad.

It's a common sight: mom at the supermarket, in the mall, at a community event, at a family gathering — anywhere — with kids in tow. Whether she's toting one child or several, her attention, her energy, her body remain totally fixated on the children. They demand it and more often than not she gives it. Everything else functions on the periphery; everything else is secondary or irrelevant. I was sad for that woman, not because she was having a bad time on a particular day, but because I knew she faced years of this kind of physically and emotionally draining attention to her children.

Mommy at Home

I first met Michelle just before she married. Young, vivacious and full of energy at the time, her life these days, some 25 years later, has become a daily grind which she can only endure with doses of Valium or Prozac.

During the early years of her marriage, she worked in a large corporation where she enjoyed a career that kept moving up. Her talent was such that she progressed from a secretarial job through several increasingly responsible positions. Michelle loved her work and the financial freedom it brought. She and her husband traveled to Europe, the Caribbean and elsewhere. Her pride in her promotions was obvious. But in those days, increasingly her conversation turned to children. Despite the obvious interest and pleasure she took in her job, she spoke as though her work simply filled time until children came along.

"I want a family." Michelle kept repeating like some mantra. That, after all, was what her life was supposed to be all about, and she said so. She took it as a given that a woman's mission was having children and that "given" hovered as a specter over her career.

At the same time, Michelle appeared to have a strange notion about what having children meant. Whenever she shopped, Michelle cut a path to the children's department and admired the cuddly outfits, the frothy dresses and the soft, flannel blankets she would one day buy for her children. She played with her nieces and nephews and took them to amusement parks and zoos, the very places she would take her own children some day. Michelle talked of traveling to Disney World when her children were old enough. Child rearing would be fun; she was sure of it. Michelle could not, or would not, see that raising children is small part fun and big part work — hard, exhausting, demanding work.

Then the corporation offered Michelle another promotion, this time as manager of a large department. She was immensely flattered and excited about the prospect. Who would have imagined she could rise so far so fast. But it scared her. Was she becoming — horrors — a "career woman?"

At that point Michelle stood back and took a look. On the one hand stood the dream job, the chance to learn, develop her talents, grow professionally, prove herself, be financially independent. On the other stood the "real" dream — family, with all its toasty warm images of babies wrapped in soft swaddling clothes, of family outings, of children paraded about in smart outfits and pink dresses, of showers of love. In Michelle's mind there was no contest. The "real" dream, the only one Michelle had known since she was a little girl when she played with dolls, won out. The dream job had somehow weaseled its way into Michelle's life, but it held no legitimacy and played no role in the vision formed for her from earliest childhood.

Michelle turned down the promotion. The time had come. She got pregnant. And the "real" dream slowly, ever so slowly, turned into a nightmare.

The first child, a boy, brought lots of joy, at least at first. Michelle doted on the baby, showering him with attention. She downshifted to part-time work, then quit her job altogether. Within a year, Michelle had another child, a girl. After the second child, she talked about having a third.

But slowly things began to unravel. Michelle's firstborn began to exhibit behavioral problems that grew increasingly worse — tantrums and rages that often erupted into violence. The little girl was no picnic either. Michelle became more and more frazzled dealing with the psychological and medical problems of her boy and the discipline problems of her daughter, brought on in part, no doubt, by the attention her brother demanded. This Michelle had *not* bargained for. This she was *not* prepared for. This was *not* part of the "dream."

The problems at home escalated. She and her husband fought increasingly about how to discipline the children. The loss of her income kept the family strapped financially. Medical bills grew. As the baby in swaddling clothes grew, he became a terror, disrupting family life night and day — a destructive tantrum, a punching episode, a fire set, a threat of suicide . . . An endless stream of trips to psychiatrists ensued, with experiments of this drug or that on the baby-turned-terrorist.

Ironically, as the years passed Michelle began to long for her job back. But it was gone, thrown away. Slowly, in Michelle's mind, work became leisure and family became work. So she cast about for any part-time job she could find as an escape from the demands of her "dream" family. Even that proved difficult. Michelle found work, but the pressures and demands on the home front exhausted her and required her to take days off here and there. She lost her job. Periodically, she made other attempts to find the right "escape" job, but it never lasted.

Along the way, Michelle had stopped talking about having a third child. Instead, she began talking about "running away from home" — a joke at first, but more and more her words took on a hard edge.

At some point, Michelle started popping Valium to get through the stress and exhaustion of her days and nights. But nothing got better. In their twenties, both her son and daughter live at home, contributing nothing but turmoil. Today Michelle stumbles along with the help of Prozac, putting band aids on each problem in turn. Life has not turned out as she planned; she is miserable much of the time; her marriage has suffered badly; and she lives with the consequences of her dream "choice."

Like so many women, Michelle bought the happily-ever-after myth of woman's mission in life. Her "choice" was really no choice at all, but a conditioned response to a lifetime of programming to motherhood. Worst, the programming came without a manual specifying what can go wrong, without a troubleshooting advice list. It came instead with a sappy image of motherhood as fun-time in perpetual Disney Land.

Mommy at Work

For most women, the picture is not so bleak as Michelle's. But it's always difficult. Navigating through life might be described as a constant, sweaty dash on a treadmill for the woman who works both outside the home and in it raising children.

Jeannine Howitz describes her experience as a new mother.[1] First she attempted, with the encouragement of an enlightened employer, to take her daughter, at age seven weeks, to the office with her each day. The experiment lasted for six months, during which time she toted her baby, briefcase and diaper bag back and forth from home to office to home. At first, she endured the oohs and aahs of inquisitive staff members (most of them single), during which time a simple trip to the copier became a social ordeal. Howitz tells of being painfully aware of her special status and of fighting hard to hide just how much time was consumed by caring for Sophie in the office:

> In a culture where women feel guilty to call in sick to work when a child is sick, it was tremendously difficult to be in an office setting, drawing a full salary, and to say, "Sophie's crying now — this phone call, this meeting, this project, whatever it is, will have to wait." In a society that expects workers to give 150 percent dedication to the job, and considers motherhood a terrible detriment to productivity, it was incredibly stressful and even painful at times to experience such a personal conflict in a very public setting when the two worlds collided.

Howitz goes on to describe how her office converted itself into a playground, with swing, play gym, walker, and toy box, not to mention the crib, breast pump equipment and mini-diaper pail. Finding her desk in the middle of it all became a daily challenge, but that didn't matter much because "it had gotten crazy, and I knew it." The growing circles under her eyes and continuing weight loss signaled a time for change. What she needed was some kind of child-care arrangement.

For the next two months, a neighbor cared for her daughter while Howitz trekked to the office. She reports getting an "unforgettable taste" of the superwoman syndrome. She rose at 5 a.m., rushed to drop off her daughter, commuted for an hour and put in a long day. After work she battled rush-hour traffic, retrieved Sophie, drove home and frantically made dinner, fed baby, cleaned her and put her to bed. After too little sleep, she did the whole thing over and over each day.

After that, Howitz packed it in. She determined to establish herself in a home-based business as a free-lance writer. That proved not much easier and she describes with humor a typical moment at home with Sophie:

> I am seven months pregnant, slithering along my kitchen floor. The ruler I clutch is for retrieving small objects lost in the dust jungle beneath my refrigerator. After several swipes I come up with a pile of dirt and a petrified saltine, so I get serious and press my cheek against the floor, positioning my left eye just inches from the target zone. I spot it — the letter "G," a red plastic refrigerator magnet. "Here it is!" I cry, hoisting myself up to offer this hard-won prize to Sophie, my momentarily maniacal toddler. Her face collapses into a sob as she shrieks, "NOT THAT ONE!"

At that moment, Sophie who is 22 months old, and in the final stages of potty training, loses it and a "gush of warm and wet" lands on her mother's outstretched leg. Wet clothes, more tears, mommy stripping off Sophie's clothes, and then her own, quickly replace the search for the elusive letter. Sophie is re-seated in her booster chair to finish eating, as her mother contemplates a dash upstairs to grab dry clothes for both of them.

Instead, the phone rings. As she answers the phone, near naked mom watches Sophie climb out of her chair and onto the edge of the table out of her reach. It's an old friend, surprised to find her at home.

"Don't you work at all anymore?"

Not if twelve to sixteen hours a day of unpaid, unappreciated labor counts for nothing!

Not What I Bargained For

The dreamy play life of four-year old mommies and child-hood dolls, of fluffy pink blankets and blue terry cloth sleepers is not the life of real mommies. The months before baby's arrival are dotted with trips to the furniture store to buy just the right crib and rocking chair, and trips to the infant department to buy blankets, carriage, car seat and crib mobiles with fairy tale creatures bouncing about. Unless, of course, she's too drop-dead sick to shop and fantasize — or too financially strapped. The romantic mythology of babies and motherhood finds its culmi-nation in the happy oohs and aahs of the baby shower just before birth. The women bearing gifts consider it bad form to bring re-ality into the picture, whatever their experiences may have been. Naomi Wolf speaks of a conspiracy of silence about motherhood and what it really entails, a sugar-coated fantasy that glorifies the "bliss" of motherhood.[2]

Much of child rearing is *not* fun. It's hard, demanding, exhaust-ing, draining work. It's work done in a child's world, not an adult's. It's work that is downright boring most of the time, involving as it does the tedium of repetitive, endless, menial tasks. The fun times, and they are there, come with a high price tag.

Children require almost constant attention, at least in the early years. And that's fine, if it's what you want. The problem is that most women can't imagine what mothering means in real time in real life until they've actually done it. In fact, given our conditioning, we have to look really hard to see this not-so-pret-ty side of motherhood. It doesn't readily show itself, and when it does, the mother myth is so strong it drowns out the reality.

The unrealistic expectations women have about motherhood are well documented. In the classic, *The Motherhood Report*, for example, researchers found that fully 70% of women (of all ages and all educational backgrounds) had "extraordinarily" unrealistic visions of what being a mother meant. They determined that women's fantasies included everything from romanticized notions to illusions of perfection — perfect children, perfect families and, of course, themselves as perfect mothers.[3] As it turns out, what women seem to really mean when they say "I want a child" is "I want a *perfect* child." But the reality check monster descends on new mothers, and it dogs them from day one.

These days the internet is awash with blog posts and status updates full of complaints about the "messy, tedious, nightmarishly life-destroying aspects of parenting," as Ruth Graham puts it in Slate.[4] Ross Douthat notes the "parental pity party" flooding social media — the internet's ever growing "Book of Parental Lamentations," the not-so-quiet desperation pervasive among parents.[5]

One disillusioned mother shared her expectations about motherhood with me. Despite being a college graduate with a major in chemistry, she confessed that "All I ever wanted to do was be a mother." She married immediately after college and had three children in the space of five years. However:

> It was not what I expected. . . It's hard to believe, but I really did think that I would be in a cottage with a white picket fence and have rosy-cheeked, adorable, well behaved children. When I was around children before I had any, I remember thinking that my children wouldn't shriek or misbehave like that! Or that it was the mother's fault . . . How could I have believed that gritty movies and even my own home was the way my life would be? . . . I had my first baby a year after marriage. He was healthy, but hyperactive with colic; cried all the time for months. I didn't know what to do with him and I cried a lot with him. That was my introduction to child-rearing and marriage and family. My husband wasn't home very much and I'm not the sort who asks for help, so I had an immense struggle to just keep going. But it took its toll and I would be short-tempered and depressed many days.

None of this is surprising, considering the "happily ever after" ending of every Prince Charming fairy tale little girls grow up with. In these fairy tales, we never see what happens in the "happily ever after" part that follows the union with Mr. Right. We're left to imagine it can only be perfect.

But how is it possible with such a high rate of divorce, broken homes, domestic violence, child abuse, single parent homes in poverty, and the like, that women have such idealistic expectations for their own mothering experience. Don't women see the real world around them, the world most of them grew up in? Yes, but most girls perceive their mothers didn't "get it right." What is so fascinating, according to *The Motherhood Report*, is that the prospect of their own motherhood presents a chance for renewal, a chance to get it right — to relive their own disappointing childhood in a happier, more perfect way. On a deeper level, the expressed desire to nurture is really about the desire to be nurtured, to be loved.[6]

As Rosie Jackson put it, consistent with the thinking of many psychiatrists, the very idea of "mother" is one that "summons up a fantasy of wholeness." This imaginary mother "represents a vision of perfection, of totality. She is the Paradise we have lost, the innocence that preceded our human experience." Jackson refers to mother as perhaps "the deepest of our nostalgic fantasies."[7] It is a small step from here to "perfect family."

However, fantasies notwithstanding, the Norman Rockwell image of family does not exist. In reality there are only imperfect individual women, in imperfect contexts, surrounded by imperfect people. So, "this is *not* what I bargained for" becomes the reality for women who enter motherhood with unrealistic expectations. Sadly, they are the majority.

The disillusionment of unfulfilled expectations stems from daily demands, both physical and emotional, that are endless. In one national study, almost half the women said that the day-to-day responsibilities of being a mother are more drudgery than pleasure.[8] Numerous authors have bemoaned the reality of birth and child care, from Jessica Mitford to Ann Crittenden to Naomi Wolf, who describes how grueling and lonely caring for a child and working can be.[9]

In the early months, exhaustion typically combines with the

tyranny of endless breast-feeding, enabled by the "nursing Nazis," as one doctor referred to those pushing this "requirement." Don't expect neutrality on this one. Advocates believe breast feeding is next to godliness, the best thing a mother can do for her child — a moral imperative.

On the other side, psychologist Elizabeth Badinter writes of the "tyranny of breast-feeding"[10] and Naomi Wolf speaks of being terribly vexed by the "Milk Missionaries,"[11] of seeing the breast feeding mother as "a cow to be trotted out of the stable."[12] She speaks of being "trapped" and irritated, of being "bored" by the endless rounds of nursing.[13] I have seen nursing moms reduced to tears and agonizing guilt for months over the difficulties of nursing, blaming themselves for "not getting it right." In any case, the nursing advocates, set loose on mothers from the moment baby makes her or his entrance, terrorize new moms into believing that if they use formula, even to supplement breast milk, they will irreparably damage their children. Yes, breast milk is better for baby (marginally so, one pediatrician told me, and let's ignore persistent reports of toxins in breast milk).

But what about mom? Is it even conceivable that maybe the incredible burden of breast-feeding is not best for mom, for a variety of reasons? Can we grant that "woman as cow" is perhaps not for every woman? But this would mean that what is good for mom would have to enter a discussion that routinely considers only what is good for baby.

One mother of two I spoke with summarized best the drudgery of it all:

> Children make constant demands. Sometimes I get so tired I just want to run away from home and stay away. But I can't. I have to go on. I get this caged-in feeling, a feeling of being trapped in my own home. It never lets up. I don't count anymore. The children always have to come first. If one of them is sick, I have to miss the presentation I'm scheduled to give at work. If one of them has a bad night and keeps me up, I still have to drag myself out of bed in the morning. My needs come last. It's so exhausting and so stressful. It's not at all what I expected . . .

The Mother-Child Relationship Turned Upside-Down

Pick your poison: "helicopter mom," "*uber*-mom," "minivan mom," "control freak mom," "total-reality mom," "muffia mom" (really puzzling to me, but apparently a cross between "muffin baking" and "mafia") . . . I myself am partial to "Velcro mom." All connote the endlessly hovering, endlessly ferrying, endlessly overwrought, endlessly catering, endlessly micromanaging, endlessly controlling, endlessly stuck-to-the-kid mom.

A big part of the mother-child relationship problem — in some quarters at least — stems from the strange notion that children should be the center of the universe, at least where mom is concerned. Somehow the idea has taken hold that mom should spend every waking moment catering to her child's needs, which, of course, necessitates that she be a stay-at-home mom. This "intensive parenting," "attachment parenting," or Velcro motherhood, means that mom almost never leaves her child's side and only engages in activities designed to serve that child. From simple feeding and cleaning, to training, to playing endlessly with the child, mom's life is completely subsumed under her child's life. The Velcro mom resists putting her child in a playpen and engages in a constant round of play group, swim group, music group, child exploration, and whatever fad of the moment is demanded of her time. In a very real sense mom's life ceases being an adult life and becomes a child's life.

This situation makes Judith Warner, in her book about motherhood, ask, "Why do so many smart, sensitive, sensible, and otherwise self-aware women get caught up in mindless and self-belittling pursuits once they become mothers?"[14] Why indeed?

This total absorption in motherhood makes for "narcissistic mommies" who endlessly foist their parenting and their children on those around them, according to Kathleen Deveny. "Just please — please — stop telling me about it," she humorously pleads. "Do whatever you want: stay home with your kids, wear gym clothes all day and make your own organic baby food . . . get your hair highlighted *while* you're in labor, breast-feed your kid till he's 17!" We didn't invent kids. Alpha Mommies need to get over it, Deveny, herself a mother, urges.[15]

It's not as though this completely child-centered approach to mothering does the child or mom any good. As Warner, along with others, has reminded us, "studies have never shown that total immersion in motherhood makes mothers happy in the long run or does their children any good. On the contrary, studies *have* shown that mothers who are able to make a life for themselves tend to be happy and to make their children happy."[16]

This phenomenon of the child as the center of the universe embodies the polar opposite of the neglected and abused child and is a destructive extreme in its own right. Historically speaking, it's a recent phenomenon. Until well into the twentieth century, children were expected to pull their own weight. In an agricultural society, children worked alongside their parents in the fields and in the house from an early age. During the Middle Ages, children were looked on as little adults, entering apprenticeship as early as age 7 or 8.

Also a recent development is the requirement that a mother should always "be there" for her child. Historically, the well-to-do home was the standard of which many could dream, although few could aspire. Everyone expected wealthy women to turn their children over to nannies and wet nurses, who occupied a domain with these children in a separate part of the house. That was the dream motherhood at one time.

By the middle of the twentieth century, in America at least, the idea took hold that the more we do for our children, the longer we do it, and the more intensely we do it, the better parents we are. In practice, of course, that day-to-day burden falls squarely on women. So we have the perverse notion that strapping 16- or 17-year-olds still need mom to do their washing, cooking, cleaning, mending, chauffeuring, and whatever. Well-being expert Carol Graham notes that this child-centric parenting, where adult autonomy is ceded to children, is not the case in other developed countries. There, "kids fit into the family; parents are in charge."[17]

Syndicated columnist and psychologist John Rosemond put it well when he said, ". . . that is the story of how parent — especially the female of the species — is now synonymous with servant." Rosemond goes on to note that there is "nothing new about mothers working outside their homes. . . What's new is guilt over doing so and — consequently — large numbers of women flogging themselves into frenzies of 'I've got to make it up to my children every evening and on weekends.'"[18]

Rosemond describes how his mother, a single parent for much of his early life, worked. Yet she never came home feeling she owed her son something. Rather, he relates, she came home feeling "I owed her something!" He owed her for putting a roof over his head, food in his stomach, clothes on his back and shoes on his feet. For her sacrifice, Rosemond's mother felt she deserved respect, obedience, peace and quiet. And, he tells us, she got it. He doesn't recall ever thinking his mother wasn't giving him enough of her time and attention.

> "By contrast," Rosemond says, "overwhelming numbers of today's kids are growing up thinking their mothers are obligated to them. Because the mother-child relationship has turned upside-down, inside-out and backward in the course of 40 years, today's child is at great risk of becoming a petulant, demanding, ungrateful brat. Unfortunately, the more petulant and demanding he becomes, the more likely it is his mother will feel she's not doing enough for him. And around and around they go, this co-dependent union of mother and child."[19]

Indeed much of the stress and exhaustion associated with child-rearing results from this cycle of physical servitude and guilt — the guilt leading to more servitude, which, in turn, leads to more guilt because the servant can never do enough. For women, it's hardly a return to a promised paradise lost.

The Road to Hell Is Paved with Good Intentions

The psychic exhaustion of motherhood can go way beyond the physical and emotional, and can last beyond the teen years. It can even exhaust a father.

Gloria and her husband, with the best of intentions, adopted a little girl from an underdeveloped country. It was the sixties. The Vietnam War splashed across the television screen night after night and with it tragic images of all those war orphans. Gloria and Harry wanted to help, to make a difference. So they determined to add a second child to their home.

When the little girl arrived at Kennedy Airport, the couple gazed in amazement at the tiny, malnourished child being carried by the flight attendant. She weighed only 17 pounds despite being three-and-a-half years old and she wore cardboard shoes and a vomit-stained dress with a patch of cloth sewed onto the front bearing their last name. When they undressed her that evening for a bath, they discovered a huge scar on her lower back the size of a grapefruit. Its origin remained forever unknown, but it surely hinted at some terrible trauma.

From the very beginning, life with Kim proved difficult. The child woke as many as seven or eight times a night, screaming out of her private pain. She fought and scratched her new parents and brother at provocations seen only by her. Ever food obsessed, Kim gathered crumbs of bread and cookies and hid them around the house against some expected hunger. She resented her brother and fought every attention given him, demanding all for herself. Even her school days went badly in the beginning. She threw toys at the teachers and fought with the other children.

In the years to come, Kim settled in, and her parents even came to call her their "little jewel." She enjoyed a good home, the excitement of travel, and parents who loved her, including an utterly devoted father who spent a great deal of time with his children.

That all changed when the terrible teens hit. During her adolescence, Kim became, as teens are wont to do, belligerent. She threw at her parents the accusation that they were not her "real" parents and should have left her in her homeland. Kim "acted out" her repressed anger (at what childhood trauma her parents could only guess, since Kim claimed to remember nothing of her orphanage days). Her parents thought they would not survive those teen years, but far worse lay ahead.

When Kim went away to college, she plunged into a new and terrifying crisis. She hated her dorm, became obsessed with unknown fears and imagined her dorm mates wished her ill. She pleaded and begged to come home. After two weeks, bewildered and disappointed, Gloria and Harry packed her things and brought her home, suspecting little of the impending emergency. The first night home, Gloria and Harry woke to find Kim standing in the darkness by their bed, raving about the neighbors who had planted a listening device in her teeth and were stalking her every move. No amount of reasoning altered her paranoia as Kim crouched in her room, shades drawn, claiming to hear voices no one else heard.

So began years with a tormented paranoid schizophrenic who careened back and forth between moments of sanity and periods of frightening madness. There were the endless experiments to find the right antipsychotic drug in just the right dose, the cut wrists, the nights when Harry slept on the floor outside Kim's room to be sure she didn't harm herself. The call from the hospital emergency room where Kim had been taken unconscious after drinking a quart of hard liquor. The frantic phone calls from Kim's friends asking Gloria and Harry to come get her — she was acting "strange." The periodic bouts of paranoia when Kim accused her parents, her neighbors, her psychiatrist of trying to harm her. The night her parents stood in the street throwing pebbles at the window where Kim had barricaded herself to get her attention, so they could plead with her to let them get her to a doctor — to no avail. The refusal of health professionals to intervene at her parents' request because "Kim is an adult." The pleadings with Kim that she take her medications whenever she stopped because she thought she was "all better." The side effects of the medicines that required her parents to rescue her.

Amazingly, through all her private hell, Kim managed to complete college, to live on her own and even to hold some jobs. But life never got any easier for her or her parents. There were the periodic breakdowns, the voices telling her she was the devil, her disappearance, the two thousand mile drive in madness that ended in a near fatal suicide attempt and institutionalization in a state far away. There were more bouts of paranoia and additional stays in mental wards, including one following a horrible period when she became convinced Gloria was trying to murder her. And the shock treatments. And the ongoing depression. There were all the financial burdens — paying for Kim's health insurance, paying her bankruptcy lawyer, paying her rent when she lost her job, periodically replacing her worldly possessions lost in this or that flight of lunacy.

These days, talk of suicide and time in the hospital to "pull herself together" have abated. The right medication in the correct dose keeps the voices and much of the paranoia at bay, enables her to hold a job and live on her own, and provides her life a measure of stability. But she remains emotionally dependent on her parents. With a daughter ever "deficient" in common sense, Gloria and Harry must facilitate major and minor decisions in her life.

Through no fault of her own, Kim, a kind and loving person, dogs them, clinging like all the walking wounded of this earth. Through it all, the burden for her parents, although immensely eased, hovers over them like a dark cloud. But certainly, they can rejoice that they "saved" a child, one who would surely have perished without their intervention.

Kids are forever, they have learned. Nor is their story all that unusual. Countless families cope with unforeseen tragedies that befall their children — debilitating illnesses, psychiatric problems, eating disorders, drug addictions, suicide . . .

Nuclear Fissures

Part of the problem lies in the nuclear family, a fairly recent historical phenomenon, although the "family-values" folks have anointed it as an absolute truth grounded in the very order of being itself. Through most of recorded history, in cultures around the world, the family was extended (and still is, in many parts of the world). In the extended family, a group of related and unrelated adults live in close proximity to each other and share in child-rearing. Indeed, it "takes a village to raise a child." In this scenario the "family" was less separate and not at all enclosed in atomic units. For women this meant, in practical terms, shared child care and many surrogate forms of motherhood. The intolerable burdens and pressures of parenting did not fall solely on one woman because there were many "mothers," and even a few male "mothers" in the bargain. Children benefited from the love, care, instruction and security provided by many "parents."

But the nuclear family is the typical reality now, whether that includes two parents and children or a single parent and children, or, for that matter, no children at all. With the displacement of shared responsibilities for child care in an extended family, the focus has shifted to one woman bearing the total burden. Too often, what was once tolerable has become intolerable, with depression and unhappiness typical.[20] Nuclear mothering takes a heavy toll on women, especially on poor and middle class women with limited financial resources. Women of means, after all, can try to recreate the extended family by purchasing the services of other folks — nannies, cooks, housekeepers, gardeners, etc.

The New Mid-Life Crisis

Motherhood doesn't always end with motherhood. Sometimes women are forced to raise their children *and* their children's children.

At age 52, Carolyn is a widow who can barely cope emotionally with her own life. But cope she must, because she is one of a growing number of grandmothers raising their children's children (more than 4.5 million such grandparents in the U.S., the overwhelming majority being women) and this is a growing trend.[21] The causes include divorce, neglect, drug abuse, teen pregnancy, death, incarceration, unemployment, and the like.

Carolyn's daughter, Alisha, a drug addict, sits in prison, convicted of felony possession of cocaine. Prior to Alisha's arrest, she bounced from home to rehab to the streets, often leaving her son, Tyrone, to fend for himself. The child's father has long since skipped, so he's out of the picture. During it all, Tyrone stayed with Carolyn on and off for extended periods while his mother tried, unsuccessfully, to get her life back on track. Now 6-year-old Tyrone is there to stay. Alisha lost custody after being charged with reckless endangerment of a child and her mother stepped in, permanently.

Carolyn loves Tyrone, but raising a second family in old age is not what she expected or wanted.

> "I couldn't turn my back on Tyrone. This is not his fault. But I wanted to be a grandmother to Tyrone, not a mother. I'm really angry at Alisha. I raised my children, sacrificed for them. I did the dirty work — changing diapers, potty training, cleaning their messes, nursing them through sickness, denying myself little things because of what they needed. That was my choice. But this isn't.

"I resent what has happened to my life. I don't want to be a mother again, not at my age. Tyrone is a handfull. I'm tired. I miss my husband. There's not a lot of money. But what can I do? Abandon Tyrone? His mother and father did that. How could I put him through that again?

"I really do love Tyrone, but I'm bitter. I don't let him see this resentment. But then I start to feel guilty about resenting the situation. I ask myself what kind of person I am that I should resent raising my grandchild. Then I tell myself that my feelings are normal. So I go back and forth between the resentment and the guilt. Meanwhile, I've got to do right by Tyrone. It's hard, really hard. I see the years stretching before me and I don't see the peace and quiet I wanted in my old age.

"My friend Lola is doing the same thing. I think *I* have it rough! She's raising her two granddaughters. Her daughter got pregnant at age 15, then had another child a year later. Lola's daughter can't take care of herself, much less those two girls. So Lola raises them. Everybody worries about teen parents and their needs. People don't think of the grandmothers who are really suffering the crisis of raising these kids."

The exhaustion and stress of raising grandchildren is not limited to the physical and emotional realms. Financial difficulties stalk many of these women. The majority, fully 57% of grandmothers raising their children's children exist on incomes below the poverty level, in tough circumstances most of us can only imagine.[22]

Where's Daddy?

So, we might ask, "Where's daddy?" in all this. With rare exception, not raising the kids! Study after study confirms that, despite the women's movement, despite the fact that most women work outside the home in some capacity, despite everything, mother still bears the sole or primary burden of bringing up baby and this is *not* getting better.[23] When it comes to practical and emotional support in the day-to-day work of the household, daddy is a big flop. Fully eight out of ten mothers report that they do far more household work than their partners, and surveyed men overwhelmingly agree.[24] *The Motherhood Report* found that three out of four mothers — the great majority — felt their mates did not provide practical and emotional support.[25] In fact, women who work outside the home do roughly 2/3 of all their family's housework[26] and they spend four times as much time dealing directly with their children as their fathers do.[27] It gets worse. Not only do men *do* less, they believe they *should* do less. Only 20% of men feel they should share the work at home, while the rest, 80%, do not think they should.[28] Studies reveal that after children enter the picture, most men actually spend *more* time away from home and at work.[29]

One of the disappointing aspects of parenthood for many is the gap between what they expected family life to be like and what it actually turned out to be. For young women, the belief that their marriages will be egalitarian, with their husbands sharing domestic tasks and parenting, has a strong hold on them. After all, times have changed, they assume! Indeed, that women believe this prior to pairing up with a man correlates with our anecdotal experience. Time and again, I hear young women assert that when *they* are married and when *they* have children, *their* husbands will share equally the household and parenting chores. (You know, the "my guy is special" routine.) They are adamant that this will be so in their cases. Sadly, it almost never is, and major disappointment sets in when reality takes over.

Naomi Wolf talks at length in her book, *Misconceptions*, about the expectation she and many in her generation had about a new model of marriage and family — a truly egalitarian match between friends and lovers. No more dad as breadwinner and mom as servant, they believed — only to find themselves reverting to traditional sex roles, especially after the birth of their child.[30]

Numerous studies reveal that after baby arrives, women and men take on traditional gender specific roles, even when both work outside the home and even in those few cases where the couple had shared domestic chores before becoming parents.[31] When a woman has a baby, her primary identity becomes mother and her sense of herself as wife and worker diminishes. On the contrary, when a man fathers a child, he retains his identity as worker and husband. He sees himself only secondarily as a father.[32] Not surprising, since women are taught to take care of others, but men are taught to take care of themselves.

Whether a woman is a high-powered executive or a retail sales clerk, she still has the primary responsibility for home and kids. As one woman put it:

> "My husband takes no responsibility for the home or children. This was not too bad when I did not work, but now that I work full-time I really have two full-time jobs. I makes me mad to have no help from him. He is only supportive of my interests and activities as long as I do all the housework, child-raising, *and* work a forty-hour week, the same as he does."[33]

The "daddy problem" reflects the cultural imbalance of power between men and women. Society confers on men the power to refuse to do housework and child care. Women have no such power. Because of their conditioning and social pressures, women cannot refuse to care for their children or do housework. It's worth noting that, historically, serving others is associated with work done by the powerless, not a characteristic ascribed to men.

Marriage and family therapist Claudia Bepko acknowledges that there are very loving men out there, men who even consider themselves feminists. But, she says, they "would never think of cleaning a toilet bowl. Most men don't see dirt. They don't see laundry in piles waiting to be folded. They're just not socialized to do housework, and don't go around with a list of responsibilities in their heads the way women do."

Even when men do see the household chores, they are masters at keeping their domestic role secondary or nonexistent because they cherish the assumption that women have an unlimited capacity for self-sacrifice. There are exceptions, of course, but men have perfected resistance strategies designed to get them off the hook, and women on it.

One strategy involves cultivating incompetence, a technique that requires men to deliberately sabotage their efforts at chores. For example, if they have to cook, they'll do it — in the most bumbling, incompetent manner — burning the rice, charring the meat, ruining the pans. It's not only "I'm too incompetent to do these menial chores," but "I'm so hopeless; I'll never get it right." Or men trivialize the need for essential tasks: "It's really not necessary to bathe the baby so often." "Why make beds; we're only going to sleep in them again?" Or they stonewall, waiting to be asked to do a chore they promised to do, until it's easier for mom to just do it. Or they plead the need to relax after "such a hard day at the office!" Or they guilt trip: "I could be out with the guys, but I'm home with my family," until he's got her feeling grateful he's around, never mind he's a slug.

Are there devoted and helpful fathers? Of course. When my children were young and my job took me on the road, my husband cooked, cleaned, and cared for the children in my absence. But the key lies in men's perception that they are "helping." Even when men do some of the work, they see themselves as "helping her out" — an expression that says it all about whose job it really is.

In fairness, women often contribute to this lopsided arrangement. In one nationwide survey, the overwhelming majority of women — 88% — agreed that it is their responsibility to care for their families.[34] (How little things change.) Many women perceive the home to be the only place they have any real power and motherhood to be a privileged status only they have. Consciously or non-consciously, they will not easily give up that "power," however paltry in reality. In many cases, women have difficulty relinquishing control. They want men to be involved, but on their terms. They want men to do the work, but according to their standards of perfection. They want men to care for the baby, but they're convinced they're the only ones who can get it right.

A letter to Abigail Van Buren captures this unfortunate attitude of so many women:

> Dear Abby:
>
> I have a problem I hope you can help me with. My husband is a terrific guy and I love him dearly. He is well-educated, clean, well-groomed, handsome and,

most important, he is a good daddy. However, he insists on "helping" me around the house with everything from diapers to laundry, cooking to clean-up, the yard work and even housework. Too good to be true?

Well, it's true, but nothing is done to my liking. The diapers are thrown into a trash can in the baby's room, not taken to the garage where they belong. The laundry is "dingy." Meals are either underdone or overcooked, and the clean-up is a "lick and a promise."

How do I tell this wonderful man, "Thanks, but no thanks."

I appreciate his efforts, but it's often more work undoing his mistakes than just doing it myself. Please help.

— His wife

She should have signed her letter "I'm Nuts!"

Another candidate for the "I'll do it all myself even if it kills me" award is Jeannine Howitz, mentioned earlier, who shares her trials of motherhood with us. She admits that she and her husband examined their options concerning child care at length. When they agreed that one of them should stay home with the baby, her husband was the logical choice since his income was half of hers and she had experienced success at her job with rapid promotions and challenging work. What's more, he was willing to be the stay-at-home parent. However, she says, "It was I who jumped at the chance . . ."[35] Go figure.

Frustrated, Frazzled and Furious

Whatever the reasons for the terrible imbalance in the work loads of men and women, small wonder that so many women are frustrated, frazzled and furious. It's not that "women are trying to do too much," according to "outlaw mom" Mary Kay Blakely. "Women have too much to do."[36]

Women's role in contemporary culture demands an enormous amount of physical and psychic energy and endurance. Women must live up to an impossible standard, one which we have unwittingly internalized: be a good "wife" for a man (even if they're living together and not married), be a great (read perfect) mother; have a successful career (on the side, of course), and kept that body looking like a twenty year old movie star. And we haven't even mentioned the 400 pound gorilla in the closet — aging parents, who are living longer and longer, and guess who's going to take care of them. One in four households is involved in caring for a loved one aged 50 and older and the majority of caregivers are women. The typical woman providing elder care is employed and spends about 20 hours a week caring for an older parent. [37]

Men don't have to live up to such a multi-faceted role. Their identity, their masculinity, is not bound in any way to the domestic arena. Culturally, the house has nothing to do with a man's masculinity. In fact, being involved with the household challenges his very sense of himself as a "man." His identity is totally bound up, still, in his work (as in paid labor). Hence, men avoid housework like a plague. It would seem that even some of those rare, but much touted, house-husbands don't like housework. One such house-husband groaned, "I don't like being centered here [at home]. It's isolating [and] it's probably harder for men because they have no acceptable role models outside the workplace." [38]

A woman's self-worth, on the other hand, is chained to the state of her home, her children, her family, her looks. If her home is not "kept up," she is not doing her job as a *woman*; if her children are not doing well, she is a failure as a *mother* (her core identity); if her body takes on too much cellulite, she has let her-*self* go to pot.

Unlike men, women are victims of Type E stress — trying to be Everything to Everybody. [39] Three out of four working women suffer from Type E stress, and a high level of stress at that. Incidentally, there is no difference in the stress rating between women who work part-time or full-time. Working part-time does not improve the quality of life. [40]

Researchers have long since determined that chronic stress may lead to serious illness and higher mortality rates because a body enduring constant stress overworks its major organs, assailing its most vulnerable areas like the heart, nervous system and stomach. The body's tendency to burn protein rather than fat when under stress results in diminished muscle tone and accumulation of fat. Stress can also lead to difficulty concentrating as well as depression and a sense of helplessness.[41]

Is the stress women feel really that bad? Yes. In one typical survey, 70% of mothers described motherhood as "incredibly stressful."[42]

Bound up in all this stress for women is the feeling of being pulled in many directions at once. Worse, women feel compelled to prove they are terrific at everything as they fly off in various tangents. Study after study reveals that the approval of others is of paramount importance to women. Hence, we feel the constant need to be everything to everybody. After all, we don't really believe it's possible for others to like us for ourselves. We certainly don't. We haven't yet figured out that getting people to "like" us isn't the point; getting them to *respect* us is.

But men could care less what others think. Their motivation is competition, winning, being "number one." When men compete, they don't think of the other guy or whether the other guy likes them or not. They want to beat the other guy! They think of themselves.

Woman: thy name is chronic fatigue. Sure, we can "have it all" — once we've taken care of the needs of our children, our mate, our aging parents, our careers and anybody else in the picture. Just don't expect to spend much time on a chaise lounge eating bonbons. As Lynn Hollyn, mother of four and business owner, put it so indelicately, "Just hope you can get some sleep in the grave, because you're certainly not going to get it in this lifetime!"[43]

Maybe we should "Just say NO!"

CHAPTER 2. HONEY, WHAT'S HAPPENING TO US?

The Impact of Children on a Personal Relationship

Marla's Story

Marla and Fred did everything together and went everywhere together. In love and obviously enjoying each other's company, they were the envy of many who knew them.

Fred had a pilot's license and on most weekends they took to the air strip that housed their small airplane and flew away to one vacation spot or another. They loved flying. Both worked and they had the money to come and go as they pleased. They also had friends, lots of them and Marla and Fred turned up at this gathering and that, interesting to be around and full of fun. As activists, both volunteered to work with their favorite social causes. It was a princess and her prince story — until, that is, their first child came along.

The transformation in Marla and Fred was slow. Marla threw herself into motherhood. She quit her job (it wouldn't be right to leave an infant, Marla said) and the couple bought their first home. In the years that followed, they had one child after another, four in all. It was painful to watch the changes that crept into the lives of Marla and Fred until they were nearly unrecognizable shadows of their former selves.

Motherhood consumed Marla. She lost weight and seemed endlessly tired. But she was the "perfect" mom, always there for her children, always cooking fabulous meals, always the ultimate caregiver. The children came first to Marla. Along the way Fred sold the airplane. Marla wasn't free to fly with him anymore. He took on more work to pay for the children who kept multiplying at his doorstep. Their community involvement had long since ended. Marla saw less and less of Fred, who, despite his growing financial security, seemed now to use work as an escape from the ruckus that had become home. Marla and Fred stopped visiting friends; there was always some excuse that centered on the children. They did virtually nothing together anymore except raise kids, and Marla pretty much did that alone.

After the third child, Marla began to show serious signs of wear, physical and emotional. She seemed nervous and unhappy, and she looked gaunt. Despite her obvious stresses and strains, Marla began talking a lot about starting her own business. Friends encouraged her to go for it, but again, despite the talk, there was always an excuse — all of them "kid excuses." Slowly, even the talk faded and owning her own business became a dream she no longer had the energy to chase, a fantasy about a future that was never to be.

Worst of all, Marla stopped leaving the house, except for emergencies. She had become, it seemed to the rest of us, agoraphobic — "tied down" to the house and its endless chores, literally. Whenever people visited, the vacuum cleaner stood in the living room, dust rags sat on the coffee table, pots bubbled on the stove — all a testimony to the unending work of housewifery.

Marla's emotional state deteriorated. She always appeared, when folks saw her, to be on the edge of a nervous breakdown. But she didn't become unglued until years later. At that point the fourth child was still very young. Marla became distraught and began seeing a psychiatrist. It was a terrible time for everyone as her passive-aggressive behavior grew in intensity. Marla's screaming bouts, arguments, and threats about leaving kept the whole family in a state of anxiety. Somehow, through it all, she kept churning out meals, cleaning the house, caring for the children's physical needs. Marla's drudgery had become so much a habituated part of her life that even in crisis she did what mommies do.

Marla's story has no happy ending. After years with her analyst, Marla accepted her state in life. Motherhood was Marla and Marla was motherhood. Her analyst "helped" her accept the status quo. So now dreary acceptance — "life goes on" — has replaced rebellion. Fred is almost never there; he's working or playing tennis with friends. It is safe to say that Fred and Marla now have a very different relationship, certainly not the lover-companion-soulmate relationship they enjoyed in their early years together. They have "settled," with their children the dominant force in their lives.

Indeed, we all get what we settle for, however little or much that may be.

Lisa's Story

Lisa married Bob in her early twenties. They met in college and after dating for two years, they tied the proverbial knot. Meeting Lisa was the best thing that happened to Bob — that's what he told everyone. He hadn't dated much before meeting her and didn't relate very well to women. His mother never displayed much emotion and "wasn't a particularly warm person," he said. In fact, sometimes he described his mom as the "ice queen." Nor was she an especially organized person. Bob remembers many a chaotic day growing up — the house in disarray, mom away a lot at work, broken appliances that went unfixed for long periods, laundry piling up till he had no clean clothes to wear, and a father very "detached" from it all.

Lisa, unlike his mother, satisfied Bob's need for warmth and order in his life. She kept a neat house, always stocked his drawers with clean clothes, cooked pleasing meals, and kept their financial house in order. Although Lisa could not be called a passionate person, she lavished her attention on Bob and they did everything together. Despite the fact that they both worked, their schedules coincided so that they came and went and met at home at pretty much the same hours. For two years they enjoyed this satisfying, if routine, marital bliss.

After two years of marriage, Lisa and Bob began to talk about children. It was time, they both agreed, to "make a family." Neither questioned the wisdom of having babies. Rather the only question was *when* to have babies. So Lisa began trying to get pregnant and within three months she had succeeded.

Lisa's pregnancy was as routine as her life, no problems to speak of and days that went by pretty much as they had before. But an uneasiness settled over Bob once Lisa actually got pregnant and he couldn't quite shake it. It was a strange sensation and he didn't understand why he felt uneasy. The decision to have a child was certainly both of theirs and he believed in his own commitment to "raising a family." Lisa, busily involved in buying cribs and flannel blankets and baby clothes, did not pick up on Bob's misgivings.

So, the "happy event" came and went and Lisa, now the good mother, threw herself into the endless round of chores surrounding the infant's arrival at home. Her attention turned from Bob to baby Carol, who demanded ceaseless care. So absorbed was Lisa that alarms still did not go off when Bob hung back from the baby. She attributed his reluctance to hold or change or feed the baby to his nervousness as a new father. Men just aren't good with babies, she thought. But even after several months, the not-so-new father still seemed uninvolved and reticent.

Bob even began to distance himself from Lisa, or maybe it was the other way around. Who could tell? Lisa became totally absorbed in the child-rearing chores and routine that didn't include Bob in the inner sanctum. So, in a sense, she had distanced herself from Bob. But Bob chose not be in the inner sanctum of dirty diapers and smelly baby, not to help, not to be involved. So, Bob had distanced himself. One thing was clear. There was a growing chasm between Lisa and the baby on the one hand and Bob on the other. It was as though they lived together but didn't *live* together. Bob had started to come home from work late — extra assignments, he said. And he started playing golf with his buddies, something he hadn't done since they married. Even their sex life did not resume in earnest long after it was medically OK. Lisa, for her part, felt exhausted at night and grateful that Bob didn't press it. Still no alarms went off for Lisa.

About ten months after baby Carol's arrival, a big alarm did go off as Lisa sorted through the pile of clothes in the hamper. She felt a piece of paper in the pocket of Bob's pants. Thinking nothing of it, she pulled out the paper. The neatly folded pink stationery gave off a sweet, floral scent that at last caught her attention, *really* caught her attention. In what must have seemed like a bad scene from a soap opera, Lisa slowly unfolded the pink paper, a sinking feeling rising in the pit of her stomach. Scrawled in bold handwriting was the message, "I can't see you for lunch. Meet me after work. Usual place. Barb."

Lisa slumped into a chair. Suddenly everything unfolded in the clearest light.

Bob and Lisa started therapy with a marriage counselor. Lisa is not sure she wants the marriage to be saved, nor is she sure Bob has really broken off his affair with Barb despite his insistence that he has. Trust, once lost, is not easily found again. But slowly the bizarre, subconscious layers of meaning behind Bob's infidelity are emerging in therapy.

What Lisa began to see was the picture of a man who married in an attempt to relive his childhood with a warm, attentive, caring mother, something he never experienced as a child. Bob, it seems, had married his ideal "mother." And for a period, Lisa filled that role by directing her warmth, attention and caring exclusively to Bob. But the birth of their child threw the whole neat scenario, and his ego, into chaos. "Mommy" had a new child who replaced Bob in her nurturing, shunting him aside, or so it seemed to Bob. Because "mother" no longer focused her warmth and caring on him, all the insecurities and fears of his unhappy childhood reared up to rattle his new-found stability. To endure "neglect" and "abandonment" a second time was more than Bob could bear, so he rebelled against his "mother" as he could not as a child. Was the affair with Barb a way of punishing his wife for "replacing" him with a child, a means of getting Lisa's attention back, or part of his own incessant search for love and stability?

Certainly Bob was not ready to have a child in his life, a child who took from him what his wounded ego desperately needed, a child who threatened all his unresolved childhood conflicts. The baggage of childhood that adults carry subconsciously works its poison in many relationships which are difficult in the best of times. Bringing a baby into the mix before that baggage is un-loaded invites disaster.

Ellen's Story

Ellen and Harry spent about three years as a married couple before the birth of their daughter. Those three years were good for them: both appreciated their professional lives, liked being together, built a home and even traveled some. By every mea-sure, they enjoyed a solid relationship built on love and mutual respect — that is, until baby Lily was born.

Ellen remembers the moment she got the terrible news from her obstetrician. Flowers from the family had begun to fill her hospital room; she was just coming out of the sedation; and Harry was sitting by her side holding her hand. Groggy and ex-hausted after the delivery, she hadn't seen the baby yet, nor had Harry. When her doctor entered the room, she knew immedi-ately something was wrong. A deep frown cut his forehead and his lips pressed together in a thin, ominous line.

When her doctor told them that Lily had Down syndrome, Ellen felt Harry's hand tighten and stiffen. Her own chest felt like a crushing weight had collapsed on her.

It was painful to look at Lily. Her narrow eyes stared out of a small head, flattened in the back and front, a head that seemed to sit, without a neck, on her shoulders. Lily's nose appeared to have been pushed into her face and her thick tongue protruded from her tiny mouth. Her body was totally out of proportion — short trunk, arms, legs, and feet. Two stubby thumbs hung from her hands and a wide gap kept the first and second toes of her foot apart. Picking Lily up felt like holding a mass of J-ello. Her limp arms and legs hung as if in mid-air without a solid anchor, flesh without muscles.

Many not-so-visible problems plagued Lily as well. She was born with a heart defect and malfunctioning thyroid and pitu-itary glands. Her skin and mucous membranes were abnormally prone to infections. Lily's parents were warned to expect severe mental retardation to match Lily's physical retardation.

The following days and months dragged into a dark parade of doctor visits and an exhausting schedule of caring for the tiny stranger in the crib, for however hard Ellen tried, Lily struck her as a stranger in their midst. Through it all, her heart ached for helpless Lily as she struggled to care for her. Ellen could not bear to commit Lily to an institution as her doctor suggested. Maybe later. Maybe. Ellen's boss had kindly given her an extended leave as she strained to make sense of it all. Suddenly the future looked very bleak.

Harry, meanwhile, was having a very hard time. Like Ellen, he was woefully unprepared for this turn of events. But unlike Ellen, he could not bring himself to "carry on." His expectations for a "family" were dashed and he couldn't imagine ever having another child, much less having a life with this child. When he tried to look into the future, all he saw was a dark tunnel with no end. He couldn't bear to look at Lily; she was the shattered glass he could not put back together, try as he might.

Being at home became more and more painful to him, so he hurried away in the morning and lingered at work as long as he could, late in the day. The weekends were the worst, for there was no place to hide. So Harry took to doing the grocery shopping, running the errands, visiting his parents — anything to get out of the house.

Ellen, meanwhile, resented being left alone to care for Lily. It seemed to Ellen that she was climbing a steep cliff carrying an unbearable weight while Harry strolled along, never offering to help with baby. But it was more than the physical strain. Harry just wasn't there for her emotionally anymore. They didn't spend time together; Lily couldn't be left. They had no sex life to speak of; Lily drained every bit of energy from Ellen. They didn't even talk anymore; the conversation always turned to Lily, and what was the point?

The strain between them grew — first in accusatory tension that hung thick in the air, then a sharp word here or there, and finally the full-blown arguments. After nine months, Harry was gone.

Martha's Story

It isn't only heterosexual couples who can be hurt by the arrival of children. Martha enjoyed a long term lesbian relationship with Becky. They lived together for years, shared a pleasant home, traveled, enjoyed each other's company and had committed themselves to a lifetime together. Both had satisfying professional lives of their own and each gave a significant amount of time to community causes.

However, in her late thirties, the biological clock thing started in on Martha. She had everything, but she wasn't a mother. Martha began to feel she must be missing out on something, that there was a primal experience she ought to be having. Although the thought of motherhood had not seriously entered Martha's head before, there it was, banging away. Even lesbians, it seems, don't escape the lifelong female conditioning to motherhood.

So Martha started agitating for a baby. Becky was skeptical. She could not understand Martha's sense that her life somehow wasn't fulfilled. So the two of them went back and forth, back and forth over the arguments for and against a baby.

Martha tried to articulate her reasons. She was getting older; it was now or never. She wanted to experience motherhood; wasn't that the essential part of a woman's life? She would love to present her parents with a grandchild; they had given up hope. Finally, Martha argued that she would love to save a child through adoption — yes, a little boy whose future would otherwise be bleak.

Becky argued against adopting anybody. She did not want to become a mother or a father. Life, she asserted, provided enough richness of experiences. How would they maintain their professional lives and their volunteer community work with a child to care for? How would they continue to travel? Lots would have to give. But more than all that, would it be fair to bring a child into a lesbian relationship? What would that child's life be like? That worried Becky the most. And the boy baby stuff? What was that, Becky chided, half serious, half in jest. Some kind of affirmation of Freudian penis envy?

Becky also questioned Martha's intentions. Was she letting her lesbian identity play a role in her newfound desire to have a baby? It's far from easy being a lesbian in this society and there's always a desire to "fit in," to be more mainstream, to prove that lesbians are just like everyone else. In a culture where being a "normal" woman is equated with being a mother, was Martha trying to validate herself, to prove to the world that she was "normal?"

But Martha remained immovable. A baby it would have to be. A male baby. So, despite Becky's serious misgivings, Martha adopted her boy baby.

Even given her enthusiasm for life and work, Martha had never thrown herself so completely into anything as she did mothering. Baby Martin became the joy of her life. Everything centered around baby. Martha gladly cleaned and fed and tended to his needs. When she had to leave for work, she missed him. Her volunteer work in the community ended. Almost every conversation, no matter with whom, or whatever the context, professional or personal, eventually turned to Martin. Martin this and Martin that. Endless photos of Martin with his teddy bear, photos of Martin crawling up a step, photos of Martin with food plastered on his face. . . Martha's colleagues rolled their eyes when Martin crept into the conversation. These same eyes glazed over when Martha embarked on a discourse about the joys of motherhood. And when the latest batch of photographs surfaced, they tried to beat an escape. Enough of Martin's teething, Martin's cute ways, Martin's eating habits. . .

During it all, Becky faded more and more into the background, until, it seemed to Becky, she was becoming invisible to her mate. Martha only saw baby Martin wherever and whatever she looked at. Becky tried to be a part of the twosome, but she somehow felt like an outsider, an intruder. When Becky tried to help with the baby, Martha stepped in; *she* would do it. The couple did nothing together anymore, as Martha obsessed endlessly over Martin. When Becky tried, ever so gently, to suggest that obsessing over Martin wasn't a good idea, least of all for Martin, Martha grew hostile and snapped at her.

After a while, it seemed clear to Becky that Martha didn't care anymore whether she was there or not. Hurt and feeling very abandoned, Becky broke off the relationship — a relationship that for all practical purposes had ceased to exist.

Diana's Story

Strange things happen when children come along. Far from being brought closer together, couples often find themselves on opposite sides of a chasm. A letter to Abigail Van Buren tells one such story.

Dear Abby:

My husband and I had our first child, a boy, last fall. We were both very happy because the baby is healthy and we had wanted a family since our marriage four years ago. We enjoyed shopping for baby clothes and furniture. My husband "Chris" was gentle and support- ive throughout my pregnancy, and was at my side dur- ing labor and delivery.

By choice, I took four months off work and only re- turned part time until the baby was older. Shortly after the baby was born, I noticed that Chris was moody and constantly on edge, but I let it pass. When it became medically possible to resume our sex life, he did not seem eager. (We have always had an active love life.)

Chris refuses to feed or diaper our child, but often complains that the baby "smells bad." He finds fault with my housekeeping and cooking. He sits in front of the television barely speaking, or "goes out with the boys" after work, which is very out of character.

He calls me "tubby" and says I should get in shape, which has almost brought me to tears. Abby, I gained only 13 pounds during pregnancy, most of which I left at the hospital. I am 5 feet 6 inches and weigh 118 pounds, less than I weighed at our wedding.

When I confronted Chris, he said he was sorry, but he no longer finds me appealing or attractive because I am now a mother! I am hurt and shocked by his words. I do not know what to do. I do not want my son to grow up with divorced parents, and despite all this, I still love Chris. Yet he has become a complete stranger. I cannot reach him.

What can I do to save my marriage?

— Diana X

It's not exactly what most women expect of Prince Charming when they have children. But it's not very unusual either.

Not-So-Wise Conventional Wisdom

Recently on the Ricki Lake Show on television, a guest admitted she had come to hate her role as mother. "I've lost love for my husband [and] my kids," she said, adding that she fantasized being divorced so she could enjoy free weekends. "Our marriage is falling apart because we have kids." After the show aired, many women wrote in to say they were relieved someone felt the same way they did.[44]

Contrary to conventional wisdom that says children bring couples closer together, the opposite is often true. Study after study has found that marriages and relationships are often hurt by the presence of children and that marital happiness decreases when children enter the picture.[45] As the years pass, the adverse effect that children have on the quality of a couple's marital relationship increases.[46]

In one national study of women of all ages and educational backgrounds, twice as many women reported that their marriages had changed for the worse after having children as those who said their marriages had changed for the better.[47] Several studies have documented in depth the severity of the social and emotional consequences of parenthood. The consensus of these studies is that fully half of all couples reported that their marital happiness had dropped as a result of having children. These couples reported more arguments and hostility toward each other, less affection displayed by their partners, increased doubts about their feelings for each other, less interest in sex, and more ambivalence about the marriage itself.[48] Yet another study found that children present a growing impediment to a happy marriage, with only 37% of marriages with children rated "very happy," down from 51% in the 1970s.[49]

Perhaps predictably, the biggest drop in marital satisfaction occurs among mothers with infants, where only 38% report high marital satisfaction, most likely because of the heavy burdens she faces in a child's early months, role conflicts, and the restriction of freedom.[50] The physical exhaustion, sleep deprivation, social isolation, hormonal changes, breast feeding difficulties, a colicky baby and other factors result in 50% — 75% of mothers experiencing the "baby blues" to some degree or other. Worse, severe and debilitating, sometimes psychotic, reactions plunge 10%–15% of mothers into postpartum depression after giving birth.[51]

Of course these kinds of dissatisfaction are not true of every relationship, and many parents experience joy and satisfaction raising children. But the negative impact of children on a couple's happiness is pervasive, and this is true regardless of education, income, religion, race, or whether a wife works outside the home or not. At the same time, numerous studies, going back decades, have shown that childfree couples enjoy a higher level of marital satisfaction.[52] One large scale analysis of 148 studies over five decades revealed that 62% of women in relationships without children have high marital satisfaction.[53]

And Baby Makes Three

Even in the best relationships, the arrival of a child, especially the first child, strains a couple in very profound ways. The "happily ever after" myth implies, but does not explicitly include, children. Prince and Princess Charming go off together — just the two of them — to build a life of intimacy meant to ensure eternal bliss. The essential component of this treasured fantasy, is the exclusivity of their special love for each other, an exclusivity that borders on "ownership." The future arrival of children exists on the periphery of this fantasy, acknowledged but not accepted for the reality it represents. That reality entails an intrusion into the exclusivity of a couple's love for each other that is often absolute in its demands, since the child's needs must be serviced. The baby's survival itself is at stake.

It is not surprising then, as psychologists have pointed out, that many fathers become jealous of their mate's attention and caring for that little intruder who seems to steal away the special and exclusive love once belonging to them. Fathers especially resent the time their mates devote to this third party who fails to know its place, and without doubt, it is an inordinate amount of time that's spent on the little one. That resentment often expresses itself in "feelings of rage, abandonment, [and] profound envy of the attention being lavished on the new baby."[54] In cases where mom is nursing her child, the problem can be further aggravated. Feeling usurped, her mate may sexually resent the child. In his mind, his lover may even prefer the sensuality of nursing to having sex with him — not an entirely idle concern in some cases.

So we have a strange scenario that frequently emerges whereby the love, time and attention spent on baby leads to deep-seated feelings of rejection by its father. Baby becomes father's rival. The trio constitutes the ultimate love triangle.

Sleeping Together, Literally

A couple's first child spells the end of the honeymoon. The presence of a baby forces a different kind of relationship on the pair, one in which the intensely passionate and romantic stage passes into history, especially if the child is born early in the relationship.

At the core of this new relationship is the different self-image each party adopts. She is now a "mommy;" he is a "daddy." These images are not entirely compatible with "lover," at least at the subconscious level. "Mother," after all, or "father," is not normally someone you have sex with. It's a new and confusing identity that requires lots of adjusting to.

The loss of sexual desire and drive after the birth of a child is well documented and the reasons are many. Fatigue is the number one complaint of new parents, especially mothers.[55] The sheer work involved in coping with an infant leaves one or both parents feeling too exhausted for sex, much less romance. Sleep deprivation also plays a role, leading to irritability and some disorientation. Mom's total absorption with baby and her concomitant "neglect" of her mate can be a real turn off. He may feel "shut out" and rejected by his wife-become-mother. The incessant demands of an infant also undermine spontaneity which, in turn, subverts sexual relations. All in all, the stress and tension that accompany the relative chaos when a new baby arrives certainly does not enhance the sex drive.

Family therapists agree that the lack of intimacy, physical and emotional, is a critical problem in long-term relationships. Good sex glues a relationship together, making both parties feel close, more understanding, more giving and even more forgiving.

But physical and emotional intimacy requires that couples have time together and talk to each other about what matters in their lives — that couples *be* together, not just live together. The birth of a child is one of the major threats to a couple's time for each other, unraveling the threads of their relationship. Nurturing the child replaces nurturing themselves.

It is not surprising, then, that this early period of parenthood is fraught with danger — anger, deviating interests, loneliness, and especially, extramarital affairs. As Masters and Johnson report, marital infidelity increases during the postpartum period. Especially for father, sexual energy, intimacy and romance flow in other directions — not a healthy scenario for any relationship.

Number One

Too often in families, as discussed earlier, baby becomes the center of the universe — numero uno — especially for mom. This happens for a couple of reasons. First, the child is utterly dependent on others for its very survival, and so demands an extraordinary amount of commitment and effort for its physical needs. A baby can literally do nothing for itself.

Secondly, the myth of motherhood in our culture assumes that the biological act of giving birth transforms a woman from a self-centered individual into a totally selfless martyr. In this new incarnation, a mother is expected to experience supreme satisfaction in sacrificing herself to the demanding creature that issued from her womb and to rejoice in endless giving. Her own feelings and needs as an adult must be denied. But that is not a problem, as the myth goes, because her "maternal instinct" dismisses all those personal needs and wants as trivial in comparison to this baby. As anthropologist Sheila Kitzinger puts it so well, "We express our infantile view of the mother as the property of the baby when we create this dichotomy between real feelings and the idealized vision of sanctified motherhood."[56] And women buy into the martyr syndrome because the alternative is perceived as being a "bad mother."

In the normal order of things, children should fit into their parents' relationship. After all, this relationship between the two people who formed the union to begin with is the core, the origin, the center of any family, not the other way around. But again and again, it *is* the other way around. Children become the center around which adults revolve and the basis of crucial family decisions. The attention centered on each other as a couple prior to baby's arrival disappears.

Ships Passing in the Night

For most parents, life together as a couple is put on hold until their children are grown. Fully three out of four mothers report that their leisure and entertainment life came to a screeching halt after the arrival of their children. Moreover, half of the mothers surveyed and 54% of the fathers say that how they spend their limited time becomes a source of conflict after having children. Women, who are generally stuck with the burden of child care and housework, resent men's leisure activities, viewing them as time away from family and a failure to help. But husbands, who see themselves as the main provider for the family, feel they deserve to play golf (or whatever the activity might be) after working so hard.[57]

More alarming, only half of all couples spend any time together without the children.[58] This, says Michele Weiner-Davis, a family therapist, is a disaster. She has found that "the number one cause of marital breakdown is that people are not carving out leisure time for each other."[59] Even in the best relationships, it is difficult to retain a close, warm, loving bond when two people's lives are like ships passing in the night. Time together alone is essential to a healthy, connected relationship.

Parents, and especially mothers, easily lose sight of themselves and their primary adult relationship. This is exacerbated by the fact that a woman's mate does not see himself, nor is he expected to see himself, in the same way as "father" that she sees herself as "mother." For her, motherhood defines her core identity. For him, fatherhood does not define his core identity — work does. Nor do they see each other in the same way. He continues to value her as wife/mate/lover while she values herself as mother. The "mother" self is primary for her; it is not primary for a man.

In putting aside their own dependency needs for the all-consuming needs of their child, a couple may well sacrifice the primary family unit — their own relationship. That relationship is the basis of the broader family unit insofar as it includes children, not the other way around. Sacrificing the adult relationship for the child cannot be in the child's interest any more than it is in their own interests. If the adult family is torn apart needlessly, the broader family that rests on that foundation is torn apart as well.

Born Yesterday

Too often, babies who should be born "tomorrow" are born "yesterday." I'm referring to babies born too soon after a relationship begins, another recipe for disaster. Studies show that the more years a couple has together before having children, the greater the odds of a marriage lasting.[60] Bonds of intimacy, love and understanding have a chance to grow and strengthen. Having children too soon derails this growth period and undermines the strength of a couple's relationship.

Bringing a child into a family precipitates a crisis, according to E. E. LeMasters in a classic work on parenthood that appeared in the 1950s.[61] His controversial claim has since been confirmed by at least 15 longitudinal studies. For 67% of new parents, the transition to parenthood leads to sharp declines in the quality of the partners' relationship.[62]

Even parents who want and plan for children find themselves woefully unprepared for the responsibility of infancy, especially the first. In one major study, caring for an infant was often reported as an unpleasant, even nightmarish experience. Infancy was the least favorite stage by far among mothers whose children were twelve or younger. Mothers with older children relate that infancy was second only to adolescence in the disliked stages of child rearing.[63]

Bringing a baby into the home has been compared to boot camp in the Marines: "[You'll] be run ragged — the food will be lousy — you'll be awakened for duty at all hours — forced to go till you drop."[64] By directing every bit of energy toward the baby, it is easy for a couple to lose sight of each other. A new and fragile relationship will have trouble surviving.

One woman described to me the strains of parenthood on her new relationship:

"Our baby was born within the first year of our marriage. Caring for the infant took so much time and energy there was almost never quiet time together just to talk or share our problems. Before the baby, we used to talk about our dreams, our future, our plans. We did interesting things together. When the baby came, I was so exhausted most of the time, I just wanted to catch a minute of rest whenever I could. I went the baby's way; he went his way. We forgot each other. How do you keep a relationship going with only scraps of time and bits of conversation? There was little sex. And romance — forget it! I regret that we didn't wait a few years to have a baby. Sometimes I even ask myself why we had a baby at all — we were happy together. Anyway, he started seeing another woman and we ended up in divorce court. Today, I'm left with my son and my ex-husband has a new wife."

Close, loving, intimate relationships are precious and they grow more precious with the passing years. Experiencing happiness together, sharing the good and bad times together, growing old together — this is one of life's most cherished gifts.

Both parties to any personal relationship must grow together and learn to adjust to each other's idiosyncrasies. We all have them. Two people sharing a life must learn the difficult art of give and take, of mutual compromise — the key word being "mutual." Consideration of the other person plays a major role in any successful relationship. A couple must spend time learning to read the nuances of the other person's words and body language, and developing listening skills. They need to learn to resolve conflicts, which are inevitable, and to support each other in times of crisis. They need to laugh, have fun and enjoy each other's company. In short, they need time together, time focused on each other.

Having to adapt to a child at the same time as having to adapt to each other is extremely difficult. One or the other, or both, adjustments will suffer. Marriage becomes much more complicated — and fragile — after a baby appears. Parents unprepared to face this jolt together will have little in common to build a future on. In those relationships where a solid foundation has been built before children enter the picture, a couple will have a better shot at enduring and thriving long term.

I'm Right; You're Wrong

Disagreements and arguments centering on children cause a great deal of tension in relationships. These strains express themselves in many ways — quiet resentment, sarcastic comments, vocal disagreements, angry quarrels and shouting matches. In these "I'm right; you're wrong" scenarios, nobody wins and relationships erode, often in increments so small no one notices until it's too late.

While many sorts of disputes exist independently of parenthood, the arrival of children often precipitates a whole range of new and unwelcome clashes. Some of these relate to the changes, real and imagined, occurring in family and personal relationships. Dad doesn't spend enough time with the kids. Mom spends too much time with the kids. Dad doesn't help with the kids. Mom is too wrapped up with the kids. He's so selfish. She's such a martyr. He neglects her. She does everything for him. He spends too much time away doing his own thing. She's trapped in the house doing everybody else's thing. He's jealous of her attention to the kids. She's jealous of his freedom. His life goes on pretty much as it always has. Her life is dramatically changed. He can do as he pleases. She makes all the compromises . . .

Some disputes center around disciplining the children. He's a pushover with the kids. She has to play the heavy. He's more lenient. She's more strict. He's spoiling the kids. She's controlling the kids. He's undermining her authority. She's undermining his authority. Frequently parents are manipulated by children. Kids learn quickly how to drive a wedge between their parents and they're great at playing them off against each other.

Often arguments erupt over financial problems precipitated by children. Child rearing is very expensive — kids suck up cash like insatiable sponges. Dad resents mom for giving up her job to stay home with the kids (or for working only part-time), forcing the financial burden on him. She resents the fact that she has no money (or less money) of her own. He feels burdened by money being tight. She feels oppressed by the financial sacrifices kids demand. Couples engage in a passive-aggressive dance. Even in cases where blaming isn't going on, the stress of too few dollars erupts with methodical certainty.

These and so many other stresses take their toll on family harmony and peace. Demands, dollars, dependency, defiance — babysitters, blahs, boredom, bandages, battles — the terrible twos, toilet training, temper tantrums — rules, restrictions, rejection. . . Even little stresses — and with children they are cumulative — tear at harmony and love.

Stranger In Our Midst

And it gets worse as children get older. Suddenly, just when it seems they are finally "growing up," adolescence overtakes them. Almost without warning, a stranger takes up residence in your home — a sullen, mouthy stranger with acne, mood swings, raging hormones and know-it-all attitudes. Just as instantly, parents become "weird," "old," "out of it," "dorky," "dumb," "inept," and "an absolute embarrassment" to be around.

Oh, and add "ungrateful" to the list of the stranger's characteristics. I watched a television report recently with great dismay. It featured the story of a teenager from a Latin American country who had been adopted as a child by a couple in the United States. At the time of her adoption, the girl, about three years of age, had been caught in the cross-fire between rebel and government soldiers. Wounded and unable to walk, apparently without any family that could be located, she languished in a camp for orphans. Eventually the girl was brought to a government agency that put her up for adoption.

An American couple opened their home to the child and took her in as their own, despite her disabling wound, medical expenses and uncertainty about her parentage. By all accounts, they were kind, loving, attentive parents who gave her every opportunity in life. All they ever got in return, however, was sullen ungratefulness that escalated to a fever pitch during the girl's teen years. She screamed and cursed at them, reminded them constantly that they were not her "real" parents, fought with her sibling, quit school, ran away from home — you name it, she did it. Throughout her teen years, she made her parents' lives a "living hell," as they say. As I watched the program, I thought of the old adages: "The road to hell is paved with good intentions" and "no good deed goes unpunished."

A television reporter interviewed this girl who reflected a total self-absorption without a stitch of gratitude for the family that had literally given her a life. She was longing for her "real" parents, not these two who had "ripped her from her homeland." For them she had nothing but blame because she didn't "belong" there. Yes, she had to admit her adoptive parents loved her, gave her a good life, cared for her — but they weren't "real."

Now, as the mother of an internationally adopted child, I rankled at the ungratefulness of this young woman. Wanting to know her "real" parents was one thing, but cursing this kindly couple and turning their lives into a nightmare for giving her a home when she had none was quite something else.

Well, the point of the story eventually got around to the discovery that, yes, her "real" parents were still alive and the television folks followed her journey back to El Salvador to be reunited with her lost family. It was a moving moment. When her birth parents were asked what they thought of their daughter's adoptive parents, they could not express enough gratitude that their daughter had been saved and given a loving home in America — in sharp contrast to their daughter's ingratitude. The piece ended on a very telling note. Ms. Sullen affirmed that, well, she couldn't see herself staying in El Salvador with her "real" parents. They were very poor and lived in a shack compared to her suddenly real American home and she didn't think she could adjust to that. So much for what's "real" and what's not and "belonging."

Ms. Sullen is certainly not unusual because she was an adoptee. Almost any parent who has survived the teen years will tell you they were living hell. Emotional turmoil and dissension rule the family during adolescence as these snotty strangers strut their stuff. Whatever marital harmony remains after years of parental stresses is taxed to the fullest at this stage. No wonder it's the period of parenting most disliked by mothers.[65] A forty-six year old mother of three describes the trauma of it all:

> "The years when they are eleven to eighteen but think they are going on thirty-five, when they think

their parents are eighty-nine and feebleminded and should be invisible, except as a source of food and money — these years are the absolute pits! Someone should invent a slumber box for parents and children to sleep through this period."[66]

But then, stress dogs teens themselves. Over the years, depression among adolescents keeps getting worse and beginning at an earlier age, with 20% experiencing depression.[67] Suicides and suicide attempts among teens have risen dramatically, with 8% of teens attempting and/or completing suicide.[68]

They're Gone! — Marital Bliss and the Joy of Motherhood

Those relationships that manage to survive long term find renewed marital bliss after getting off the parenting treadmill. Children do eventually leave. They certainly do not build their lives around their parents — a point we should remember when we're tempted to center our lives around them.

When children finally leave home, the "empty nest" fills with peace and quiet. But the myth of the empty nest states that when children grow up and leave home, mothers suffer from feelings of uselessness, loneliness and depression. No indeed! The reality for most women is quite different. Mothers report an overwhelming feeling of relief at their newfound freedom from the responsibility of caring for their children. Only 5% unequivocally wish their children were still living with them. Roughly half of empty nest mothers responded to the question, "Do you wish you still had children living at home?" with, "Definitely no!"[69] The most commonly cited advantage of children fleeing the nest is the fabulous feeling of freedom. Women relish their newfound sense of independence.

That sense of freedom plays out in a couple of ways. For some, the couple's relationship continues and they stay together for as long as they live, happily or unhappily. For others, the departure of children from the home precipitates a divorce. When couples find their relationship devoid of anything besides the children, for whose well-being they stayed together, they often split. The divorce rate of empty nesters over age 50 has more than doubled in the last 20 years. Recently, 1 in 4 couples divorcing are over 50 years of age whereas in 1990 it was only 1 in 10.[70] What's even more interesting, women initiate two-thirds of all divorces after age 50.[71]

Why don't these women want to be married anymore? I think Jane Glenn Haas, syndicated columnist on issues relating to older people, gets it right when she says, based on her own research, that women want independence. They "don't want to be subservient; they value independence; they have not made good relationship decisions in the past; they feel men want control; they don't want to be 'a nurse or a purse.'"[72]

The toughest thing about the "empty nest" is not missing the kids, it's adjusting to one's partner. "Now what?" emerges as the biggest question for couples whose lives have revolved around their children to the exclusion of themselves. The move from child focus to partner focus slaps many a couple into the cold reality that they have little in common and no strong bonds with each other. Their sense of self-worth has so wrapped itself around children that their vulnerability as a couple escalates.

One woman put this vulnerability vividly in describing to me the aftermath of her empty nest.

"It's awful. It hit me how little we have in common what with the children grown and gone. I had spent all those years focused on the kids and their needs. Fred was always there, in the background at least. We traveled with the kids. We went out to dinner with the kids. If we saw a movie, it was a children's film with them. I quit a job I loved to be home with them. I didn't see it then, I was so wrapped up in their lives. Fred and I were mom and dad. I don't know when we stopped being friends and lovers or when we stopped sharing adult things together. We did very little together, just the two of us.

"Now look at us. We don't have anything to say to each other. We don't know how to be together without the kids around. If we talk, it's about how the kids are doing or what we'll do when the kids come home to visit, which they seldom do. It's scary. It's like we've disappeared. We left with the kids. I know that doesn't make sense. It sounds crazy. We're here! But somehow we're not here. How long do we go on like this? I hate to admit it, but I have fantasies about leaving, starting all over."

For others the "empty nest" is an opportunity. It offers many advantages, the biggest being that the marriage improves. Bringing children into the home strains relationships; getting them out of the home eases the strain. In one national study, when asked whether their relationships got better, worse or stayed the same after their children left, the majority of mothers reported that every aspect of their relationship with their mates changed for the better. The most frequently stated changes for the better involved the improvement of the quantity and quality of time spent with each other and a definite improvement in their sex lives.[73] Just as the introduction of children into a relationship frequently decreases marital happiness, the exodus of children from the home often marks a rise in marital happiness.[74]

Here's how another woman shared her experience in the empty nest:

> Things are so much better between my husband and me since the kids left home. We hardly ever argue anymore and we do lots of things together. We are more affectionate to each other and our sex life has definitely improved. I should say we have one now that we don't have to listen at the door or sneak around for a moment together. And we talk to each other! The TV isn't on all the time. We watch what we want to watch. There's no hard metal racket filling the house. And nobody's telling me they're hungry all the time and there's no food or asking that endless question, "What's for dinner?" If I don't want to cook, I don't. We just go out to dinner together. We've got more money now for the things that are important to us and we don't have to scrimp with every penny because the kids need this or that. But I'll tell you, most of all it's the freedom. I haven't felt so free in almost a quarter century!

So, one is tempted to ask, what was the point?

It's a question Judith Warner has asked herself many times, for all her wisdom about motherhood.

> I wish I could say that I knew. I wish I believed that this game we all play actually has an end, or a point, or some value. Some higher purpose. Some meaning. Something to justify all the stress and mess that we impose these days on our children and ourselves.[75]

CHAPTER 3. MOM'S TALENTS DOWN THE DRAIN

The Impact of Children on Career and Livelihood

That's Life

Work is critically important in every human life. Ideally work entails the realization of each person's talents and skills as expressed in what they do. Each human life is complex and capable of being lived on many levels, physical, emotional, social and intellectual. The more constrained an individual life, the less it can enjoy and express the fullness of its humanity.

Moreover, so far as possible, everyone, male and female, has an obligation to contribute something to the broader community since all of us benefit greatly from community. Human life depends on a functioning community — its ability to provide food, shelter, security, healthcare, education, transportation systems or any of the endless needs that we cannot provide for ourselves as individuals. This obligation includes, but goes beyond narrow self-interest, beyond narrow concerns for one's own nuclear family.

So, work is important for two reasons — so that the individual can attain a meaningful and fully human life and so that the individual can contribute to, and derive benefit from, the larger community of which he or she is an integral part.

A Mother of the Future — Almost

A rising star. That was the cliché everyone used when referring to Rebecca, who was anything but a cliché. I met her when she directed a newly created department. A young woman in her early thirties with impressive credentials, everything about her was a class act. Confidence oozed from her very being. Articulate and authoritative, everyone respected her. Rebecca spun out creative ideas, implemented vital programs, and led a diverse staff through the early growth years of her department.

But she wasn't only good at what she did, Rebecca loved what she did. Her career was a perfect match. An activist at heart, she established programs that made a difference in the lives of young people. The impact of her department's programs was widely felt. Exciting work filled her life and her contagious enthusiasm reflected itself in the way she carried herself, the way she spoke and the way she worked. I knew her for some years in this capacity and watched her professional growth and the growth of her department as one watches an obvious role model. She was the consummate career woman, full of life and energy, full of creativity and ideas, full of vision and promise. There was "no place for her to go but up."

Personally, Rebecca seemed equally successful. She had built a solid, happy marriage, a true partnership of equals, and she often spoke with pride of her husband.

Then Rebecca became pregnant. When I heard, it struck me that she was the last person I'd have expected to have children. I don't quite know why I thought that. Perhaps it was the don't-tempt-fate thing (i.e., You've got everything going for you. Why tempt fate by adding children to the mix?). Or maybe it was the don't-you-know-what-you're-letting-yourself-in-for thing (i.e., Are you crazy? Where will you find time and energy to raise kids?). Or maybe I just wanted her to be different, not to fall into the "apple pie and motherhood" routine all the rest of us had bought and paid a price for. But she wasn't operating on my agenda.

Indeed, Rebecca explained at length that she and her husband were determined to share equally the role of nurturer for their child — a grand experiment — actually, the ultimate experiment in gender equality! She would not be a traditional mother who shouldered the whole burden of child-rearing. On the contrary, she and her husband would make strictly equal accommodations in their careers. That meant both of them would move to part-time status at their jobs after the child's birth so they could share in raising the infant. Rebecca expressed confidence that no one's career would suffer, and if any career was to suffer, it would be both careers. Fair is fair! This was concept equality at its most ambitious.

So for the next nine months, Rebecca lumbered under the increasing weight of the baby within — that part couldn't be made fair. When she had the baby, Rebecca and her husband did, indeed, move to part-time status. Because she was no longer a full-time director (though she was still director), her staff took over pieces of her work. But reality, after all, settled in and there was no way to stretch fewer hours to handle the work she had been doing. As months passed, Rebecca increasingly slowed her pace, and more and more of her work went to others. Slowly, it seemed, she was becoming director in name only.

When I saw Rebecca again some months after the child's birth, her appearance shocked me. A frantic quality had replaced the calm, in-control-of-myself-and-my-work quality that had set her apart. She showed the strain of juggling a child with her high-powered duties. Perhaps that strain was not physical, but emotional — I don't know. Anyway, her face looked wane — haggard almost — and devoid of its old spontaneous, care-free look. Others commented on how "terrible she looked." Her confidence had evaporated, at least on the surface; she did not strike me as a happy camper.

Meanwhile, the staff people around Rebecca appeared resentful, and small, oblique grumblings crept into their conversations. At one meeting I attended, the tension exploded into open hostility, undermining her authority. In a classic case of I'm-losing-control-so-I'm-going-to-exercise-more-control, Rebecca began to act like a traditional boss, imposing orders where once she had lead by consensus. After the meeting, two people voiced strong objections about her leadership to me. Somehow, along the way, dissension had found its way into this well-oiled and cooperative team.

I found out later that the grand experiment Rebecca and her husband had embarked on to establish equality in child-rearing had pretty much gone the way of other such well-intentioned notions. Her husband had been offered a promotion, but only if he resumed full-time status. It was, as the argument goes, "too good to pass up." So there was Rebecca, experiencing a difficult infancy (baby cried a lot and had some unnamed problems) and dealing with it as women had always dealt with it — herself. A few months later, I heard that Rebecca had left her job altogether and become pregnant with a second child.

There it was — hubby moving on and up with his life and profession, mommy moving back home and abandoning a brilliant, promising career, not, apparently, out of choice, but because Rebecca had been naive about the impact of motherhood and her ability to obliterate thousands of years of patriarchal tradition. After that, she seemed to drop out of sight and when I asked about her some years later, I was told she was doing "a little consulting" while raising her children.

Some argued she had made her choice and after all, wasn't that what feminism was all about. Maybe it was about choice. But more likely it was about centuries of tradition and culture that dictate what women can and cannot do.

Rebecca's story is not unusual or particularly extraordinary. While not many women embark on the "grand experiment," they've had to make some form of accommodation in their careers, to interrupt them, or to give them up altogether when they have children.

A Mother of the Past

I met Liz, an older woman, in a seminar I was teaching for re-entry women — displaced homemakers and others — seeking to come into the workforce after having raised families. Liz hung back one day after class. I could see she was troubled about something, so I asked if she was OK.

"I'm sad," she answered. "Incredibly sad."

I asked her why.

"Because I never realized these things before, when there was time." Liz went on to lament her "wasted life" — her words.

It was the darkest moment in all my years of teaching. Few

tragedies are greater than when a person believes she has wasted her life. Life is short and we don't have an infinite number of chances to get it right.

An extremely bright woman, Liz grew up in South Africa during the turbulent years of apartheid. A socially conscious activist, she worked with an organization of white women laboring to end apartheid. Liz, a teacher by training, chose to work in a black township educating black children, a gutsy and dangerous thing for a white woman to do at the time. Her face beamed as she spoke with pride of her work among the children in the terrible poverty of that township. Art was one of her strengths and she used it to help the children give expression to their hopes and dreams and to build their self-esteem, which they had precious little of. Clearly, Liz had loved her work among the poor.

The story of her move to the United States was not clear. Whether Liz came because she married or she married after she came, I never did find out. What was clear is that she and her husband settled down and raised a family, or rather Liz did. Her husband pursued his profession while she stayed home to nurture their offspring. Those years, looking back, now appeared to her as "wasted." It's not that she didn't love her family — she did. But *her* life stopped, for all intents, as she ministered to her husband and children's needs. Liz did not pursue her teaching, activism, or any other career; she did not grow professionally; she did not develop her artistic talents; she did not "fulfill" herself. She serviced those around her as they were busy fulfilling themselves.

Then suddenly it hit her. What had she done with her life? Where had it gone? What was that gaping hole, more than a quarter of a century, in her life?

So Liz found herself in her "golden years" without meaningful work, without professional skills, without credentials, without money of her own. To her, "fulfillment" through children seemed fraudulent in retrospect. She had bought the line only to find it wasn't worth much. The fact that she had earned no money of her own seemed to insure her inability to salvage her life. Liz wanted to go back to school, to pack a lifetime into her senior years, but she had no capital of her own. She was reduced to a supplicant, seeking to convince her skeptical husband to subsidize her and by looking for grants. No wonder an incredible sadness settled over her.

Liz's story is told in countless women, over and over. The details are different, but there it is — the middle aged or older woman who gave it all up for motherhood, only to find disappointment, despair, powerlessness and, often, poverty at the end. While we like to think that has all changed with young women today, sadly it has not.

A Mother of the Present — Out of the Workforce

Jane was only 29 when she suffered the indignity of trekking back home to her parents half a continent away, two small children in tow. Her husband, a college professor, left her for a student in one of his classes — without warning, at least that Jane had seen. In the end, that she had been the "perfect" wife and mother for over seven years meant nothing.

Jane had done the "right" thing, or so she thought. She wanted children and believed she had to give up her job to "bond" with them — a strange and trendy concept with no scientific basis[76] — that treats motherhood like a postage stamp that must stick to an envelope to reach its final destination. Well, "bond" she did. Jane quit her job and became the quintessential mother raising her "two darling girls," as she referred to them. She lived for her family — decorating her nest, caring for her babies and hosting her husband's academic gatherings. Jane threw herself into domesticity with the kind of blissful abandon young women talk about these days when they affirm, "My family comes first" — presumably failing to add "And I come last."

The day her husband walked out, she dragged herself out of her broken nest to keep a volunteer commitment. When she arrived looking dazed, ashen and puffy-eyed, a friend took her aside.

"Jane, are you all right?"

Tight-lipped and grave, she whispered, "Larry has left me. I don't know what to do."

Jane *really* didn't know what to do. For weeks she sat paralyzed at home with the girls in some desperate belief that Larry would come back into her life as quickly as he had left. When he walked, Larry had given her a few hundred dollars — not even enough to pay the mortgage — and had suggested that she needed to "go back to work." Jane could not even bring herself to call a lawyer. Some days she could not get out of bed. As the weeks dragged on and the bills piled up and the girls whined for daddy, Jane's stupor slowly lifted. A decision had to be made. Her prince had become a frog.

Her friends urged her to go back to work, but the years had transformed her former job in a technical field. Decorating her nest, playing the social hostess and "bonding" with her two darlings hardly qualified her for a return to a job she no longer understood. Eventually she contacted a lawyer, packed up the girls and some belongings, and headed west to her childhood home and her parents.

What became of Jane, I don't know. Demoralized, she would have to find the courage to start life over, this time with two small children — the "family that came first" — to reckon with. The career she left behind was not forgiving.

Another Mother of the Present — Out of the Workforce

Unlike Jane, Martha did not get left by her husband. A high-powered lawyer, she made more money than her husband, also a lawyer, and had an exciting job at a prestigious law firm. A few years into her work she determined to raise a family. After her first child, she began to work part-time. After her second child, she left work altogether to be with the children. Soon a third child appeared. She did try briefly at one point to go back to the law, but found it too much.

Over the years I watched the visible transformation of Martha. A bright, confident woman slowly morphed into a doting — and frazzled — mother/baby-sitter/nanny/nurse-maid/cook/cleaner... Instead of dealing with clients and case law, her ever-present children reduced her to a person constantly caring for the most trivial and most important of their needs. It was painful to see the look of constant stress on her face, the frantic coping with three active and rambunctious children, the endless running here and there to tend to their all-consuming needs. Martha's very appearance changed as she looked more and more haggard and older each time I met her. The last time I saw her, at a wedding, she was chasing one or another of the children and angrily asking — actually demanding — her husband to "help me with them."

The years passed. She never returned to the law, validating the argument against hiring women for important positions —"they'll have children and leave" — to the detriment of all women. Her children will be grown someday and how she will look back on her life is an open question. She may be very glad she made the choice she did — or she may not.

A Mother of the Present — In the Workforce Part-Time

I see these "Janes" everywhere, bright-eyed and naive. Their story lines vary in their sameness. One young woman in a seminar I taught raised her hand. I can't remember her name. We were talking about differences in the workplace and how others react to those differences.

"I work part-time," she proudly affirmed. "And others are jealous."

"Jealous?" I asked.

"Yes. You see, I'm fortunate. I don't have to work full-time. My husband makes enough money to support me and I can spend more time at home with my son. The people around me wish they were so lucky."

Bubbly and earnest, she said it in perfect innocence, in complete oblivion, in blatant ignorance of her vulnerability. There she sat, steeped in the Prince Charming myth, elevating dependency to a virtue and claiming it was what everyone else wished for. That she had become a financial ward of her husband and was reverting to the state of a dependent child, turning her partner and lover into her father, she utterly failed to see. She didn't have to worry about a fast track or a slow track or any kind of track. She was derailing and didn't know it.

A Mother of the Present — In the Workforce Full-Time

Another woman I knew chose teaching as her career for the sole reason that it would allow her to "work around" her family. Barbara could be there in the morning to get them off to school; she could get out of work in time to greet their school bus; she would have holidays off to be with the kids; she could spend summer at home when her children were not in school. What a great plan! Except that Barbara became more and more miser-able as the years went by.

A creative, artistic person, Barbara had given up her first love, art. As a college student she had dreamed of a career in graphic design and advertising in a large urban setting. She loved big cities and all their excitement. Barbara had won a number of awards for her art work and her instructors spoke of her "great promise." Giving up the career she wanted hadn't seemed like such a big deal when she married her prince. She was in love and full of the excitement of planning a family. But as the picture of her dream family moved to the forefront, her life and her work moved further and further out of the picture.

Over time, the small town she lived in felt deadening and Barbara came to hate teaching and, to her, its mind-numbing routine. Stifled by rules, regulations, daily lesson plans, and bells that rang every 40 minutes, she felt her creativity and en-thusiasm drain away. Surrounded by little children at work and at home, Barbara missed the intellectual, cultural and political stimulation she had loved as a student and expected in her work. Her career as a teacher fit her family just fine, but it didn't fit her.

A Mother of the Present — In the Workforce Full-Time, Sort Of

Lori has it made. That's what her friends think. And if you ignore the damage she is doing to other women, she does have it made.

Lori holds a medical degree. A number of years ago, she was interviewed by a group of male doctors in a practice in her field. The practice was a prestigious and profitable one and their offer for Lori to buy in as a full partner thrilled her. When they made the offer, they shared with Lori the rules of the practice designed to ensure that everyone pulled their weight and everyone was treated fairly. At the time Lori had a small daughter and a son and she accepted their offer without qualification and without any indication that she could not abide by the rules.

Once on board, however, Lori proceeded to operate on her own agenda without regard to her partners, their needs, or the rules. Her agenda: my family comes first. Now this is fine, but she didn't say this when she signed on. Coincidentally, "my fam-ily comes first" is not an agenda her husband, also a doctor, operates on. He flatly stipulates that the children are her responsibility and she accepts that. She is the quintessential doting mom who wants to "be there" for her overindulged children.

The consequences of her approach routinely wreck havoc in the practice and have led to bitterness. If a child is sick, Lori calls in to cancel her scheduled appointments although she has a nanny who cares for the children while she's at work. This means patients must be rescheduled or someone else must cover for her in addition to doing their own work. She also leaves work early if the children need something and routinely takes personal calls from the children when they want to "talk to mommy." Since these situations are not occasional occurrences, the extra burden on her partners is ongoing.

The problem not only affects her day-to-day work. Although the rules specified that everyone would take a maximum of six weeks vacation a year, Lori always takes at least eight since she wants to spend as much time with her children as possible. In practice, "my family comes first" means that Lori expects and demands special privileges and special treatment because she is a mother. It means her partners get imposed on and her patients get catch-as-catch-can for a doctor — not to mention the possibility that her male partners would also love to spend less time working and more time with their families.

Now we might reasonably note that the "rules" were made by men for men and to accommodate the needs of patients, not to deal with the needs of mothers. Yes, but it's one thing to try to change the rules to accommodate the interests of a mother, and something quite different to simply flout the rules after agreeing to abide by them.

Yes, Lori "has it made" because, as a partner, her colleagues cannot touch her. And she knows it. The problem is the damage she is doing to other women by feeding into the classic stereotype of the uncommitted working woman: Her family comes first; her work comes last (as though it were not possible for *both* to be important). Lori's partners grumble among themselves and vow they will never hire another woman.

Like Rebecca, Liz, Jane, Martha, Barbara and Lori, most women still accommodate their careers — indeed, their lives — to motherhood. And there's a high price to be paid. Rebecca

badly misjudged her ability to juggle a high powered, challenging position with the demands of motherhood, not to mention
her expectation that sex roles could easily change. In Jane's case,
she found herself suddenly and desperately needing the job she
had turned her back on. Liz discovered herself, in later years,
disappointed and saddened by the loss of her aspirations and
dreams and frustrated by having no money of her own. Martha
abandoned work she loved, only to find herself increasingly har-
ried and frustrated. Barbara compromised her life, her talent and
her creativity, thinking she was only compromising her time.
Lori "had it all" — at the expense of others.

Hitting the Baby Ceiling

OK, I can hear the shouting out there. "So what! Children are
important. What's wrong with a mother sacrificing her career?
What's wrong with full-time motherhood, for a period of years
or permanently, if it comes to that?"

Plenty is wrong! And women need to start looking at what's
wrong realistically and unsentimentally.

For openers, a woman who does not earn her own keep, or
who works part-time and cannot support herself on those part-
time wages, is vulnerable and at the mercy of someone else's
good will — a husband, a partner, parents, public assistance (i.e.
mean-spirited politicians), or whatever. *To be an adult dependent on
another person for the necessities of life — food, clothing, shelter — is as
bad as it gets.* Can a woman easily leave a batterer, a philanderer, a
verbal abuser, a domineering or emotionally distant mate if she
and her children depend on him for food, clothing and shelter?
Can a woman think and speak freely if what she says challenges
and disagrees with the man who feeds, clothes and shelters her?
On the contrary, pleasing and indulging "big daddy" becomes
the imperative.

How does it feel, really feel, not to have a dollar that's truly
one's own? I can't count the number of times a woman has told
me, bitterly, later in her life, that her husband considers the
money accumulated as his money, not theirs, and certainly not
hers. Or he assaults her with the accusation that she did not contribute to their savings and investments.

Recently a self-absorbed male acquaintance spouted on

about how he had "given" his wife a beautiful home in their retirement. It never entered his mind that she had equally contrib-
uted to his success by entertaining his colleagues, by helping
with his work, by leaving the workforce to raise their children
("his" children, he calls them), by later working only part time
to tend their home and family. This is a man who, by his own ad-
mission, has never washed a dish or laundered his own clothes. I
remember the times she wanted to do things around the house,
fairly simple things like put in new carpeting, but he would not
approve. Everything she has, he sees as "given" to her by him.

Nor can a woman count on the relationship — and her financial security — continuing. The divorce rate is 50% overall for
first marriages, 60% for remarriages.[77] When a divorce occurs,
apart from the emotional trauma, financial devastation routinely
hits women and their standard of living drops dramatically.[78]

Of course many partners never marry; they cohabitate. But
an even higher instability marks these relationships and, overall,
cohabitating couples are roughly five times as likely to separate
as married people.[79] Add in the death or disability of a husband
or partner and the picture is even bleaker. The stability of family
life, whether defined by marriage or cohabitation, sits on shift-
ing sands.

In divorce we wrongly assume that alimony and child support will pick up the slack. Typically the husband has more
money to pay for a better lawyer. Only 60% of custodial parents, overwhelmingly women, receive a child support or alimony
award which legally *entitles* them to financial support. And being
entitled to support is not the same as *getting* that money. It gets
worse. Men pay a median amount of $3,600 annually to support
their children. And even that pittance is not paid regularly, with
only 45% of custodial parents getting every support payment
due.[80]

If I were a betting person in divorce situations, the last person I'd put my wager on is the woman. When women put themselves in a situation of financial dependency where the odds are
better than 50-50 against them . . . I'll be kind and say it's just
plain naive.

The term we use for women left behind when daddy is gone,
whether through divorce, separation or death, is "displaced

homemaker" and it's not pretty. I've seen these women up close. I've worked with them as they drag their children to career semi-nars and training programs, hoping against all odds that they can repair the irreparable damage done to their careers and lives. I've listened to their tearful stories — all the same in their differ-ences — that invariably end with some version of "How could I have been so dumb?" Or, "I don't know what I was thinking." Or, "I *never* thought it would happen to *me!*" I remember the woman who kept saying to me, "But we were *so* much in love. How could he do this to me?" He could and he did. The "how" is irrelevant.

The Loss that Keeps on Losing

Being out of the job market, even for a period, hurts a woman economically. Not only is her pay cut dramatically or totally by a move to part-time or drop-out status, she will pay economically for the rest of her life. Even if she does return to the job market, with rare exception her pay will not catch up to what it would have been had she stayed the course.[81] Worse yet, she will suf-fer economically in her most vulnerable years when she tries to retire. Her lower wages over the years will negatively impact her savings and pension, if she has managed to build them at all, and her social security income will be lower than it would have been had she kept working.

Overall women are 34% more likely to be poor than men, but older women are 73% more likely to be poor than older men in the United States.[82] The median income of an older man is almost twice that of an older woman.[83] Motherhood has a lot (though by no means everything) to do with that fact, especially when women opt out of the workforce, downsize to part-time work, or jump in and out of the job market.

What's more, a woman's chances for advancement in her chosen field will suffer if she leaves her job, even temporarily.[84] Her skills and talents atrophy and she will bear the stigma, fairly or unfairly, that she put her family first. In a workplace as male-oriented as ours, a "family first" value will earn a woman a swift kick off the career ladder. The baby ceiling is alive and well.

Finally, the loss of adult stimulation is cumulative over time. Spending a significant portion of one's life in four walls with little children wears thin really quickly. Sure, kids are cute and fun and adorable, but they are also hard work (menial work) and children are totally self-centered. Being with children literally means being with the most self-absorbed and selfish little folks in the world. I say that *not* as a criticism. It's simply the reality of that stage of human development; we were all there once. As many parents will testify, too often children in this culture stay self-absorbed clear through the teen years! Children are simply not capable of providing intellectual stimulation the way being around adults can.

And, it's probably not much better for a child to be stuck with one person — mom — all or most of the time. Kids need diversity and people and different stimulations too. Self-reliance and independence, valuable traits parents are obligated to develop in their children over time, do not automatically spring forth in the child smothered, pampered and over-protected by mom.

Now, something of an argument rages about whether mothers choose to "opt out" of the workplace or are forced out by inflexible workplaces not designed to accommodate mothers. Of course, the capitalist workplace abhors any *serious* suggestion that it should adjust to family, motherhood, or personal lifestyle preferences, with a few notable exceptions. (Yes, lots of lip-service floats around.) Those endless books and articles that offer companies plans, policies and strategies for adapting itself to "family" lack a fundamental understanding of the nature of capitalism. It adapts to only one thing — profit, and the more the better. It will do almost anything to make a profit. It boasts a long history of sacrificing and exploiting people for profits. Its goal is profit. *Not family.* The fact that companies have been urged for decades to adapt to the family needs of its female workers, and have not in any substantial way, speaks volumes.

In the end, the argument hardly matters. Women leave because they are mothers, regardless of whether they choose to leave or leave because the workplace won't accommodate their motherhood. Roughly 43% of women in the United States leave their jobs, permanently or for an extended period, when they have children.[85] Many, although certainly not all, are well-educated, higher income women. Women earning low wages do not typically have this luxury.

Another study of college-educated women found that more than half had chosen a "nonlinear" career path when becoming mothers, that is, they made career choices that allowed them to spend more time with their children. Of these women, 38% took a position with fewer responsibilities and lower salary than they were qualified for; 36% moved to part-time work; 25% reduced the number of hours within their full-time job; 16% declined a promotion.[86]

Consistent with the much maligned "mommy track," study after study reveals that women pay a high price for motherhood.[87] That price is paid in lower wages, fewer promotions, part-time work, fewer benefits, lower retirement savings, loss of pensions, less social security, added discrimination in some form, diminished educational opportunities, not being taken seriously professionally, and financial dependency or outright poverty.

In short, the cliché is right — it's really hard to "have it all," at least if you're a woman, which does not mean we shouldn't keep trying. *But, if we're going to choose motherhood, it better be with a clear, unvarnished view of the price tag.*

A Recipe for Disaster

Beyond the economic penalties, the most important point to be made lies with the concept of personal development and meaningful work. We use the term "career development" as a kind of ornament some women wear in the workplace, a luxury reserved for the well-educated and the ambitious. In fact, career development (a very inadequate phrase) is much broader and is relevant to everyone. It refers to the process of creating ourselves through work, developing our talents and skills, learning new things, growing in our work, expanding our intellect and sensibilities, relating more and more effectively with people and moving to ever more challenging heights. Without career development we stagnate, doing the same work over and over in a mindless monotony that deadens the spirit and the mind.

Ah, yes, I can hear the indignant protests: "Raising children is meaningful work!" I agree, but that misses the point. While raising children is important work, it is one human function among many. The problem is that women make motherhood the center of their lives and equate it with who they are. *It's disheartening in the extreme that so many women today are buying into the "biology is destiny" mandate* — a mantra that has for millennia stripped women of full human status, resulted in women being treated as lesser beings than men, subordinated women to men, robbed women of leadership potential, confined them to the domestic sphere, and made them financially dependent on men.

In fact, each person is a complex set of talents, skills, and ideas in the making — a formless mass of possibilities. Having babies is a strictly biological function, something almost anyone can do. Raising children is the process of *helping another human being* learn to live in the world, to find meaning and to create herself or himself. *It does not create me, the mother.* As a human being, a woman is still obligated to develop her own person, to grow, to learn, to create meaning in her life, to nurture her self-worth. Women who put their lives on hold, or push their human needs and potential into the background, or live their lives through others, are abdicating their own lives.

Taking responsibility for another human life and abandoning one's own is a recipe for disaster. Loving and caring for another person, child or adult, should not necessitate abandoning or "wasting" my own life. Motherhood should not be like taking crack cocaine — enjoying the high while it destroys my life.

Motherhood as Escape Hatch

A "career," whereby I develop my unique self in meaningful work and support myself financially, is not an expendable option for women any more than it is for men. Since we are active beings not passive ones, meaningful work is the stuff life is made of.

Now, the point is frequently made that women, who so often toil at menial jobs, leave work to have babies precisely because their work is *not* meaningful. Yes, but that is a cop-out and a very bad reason to have a child. A child is too precious to be used as an escape hatch. If a woman does not have meaningful work in her life that develops her mind and talents and skills, the answer is not having babies. The answer is to find or create meaningful work. But that requires courage, discipline and, especially, a strong sense of self-worth, something is short supply among women who are "told" from birth that they are less than men.

So, far too many women use motherhood as an escape hatch. But escape from what? From dreadful, monotonous work, from the demands of a career on the fast track, from fear of failure, from fear of success, from taking responsibility for her own life, from independence? Women run from disillusionment with the world of work to the comfortable cocoon of home, the comfort of four walls where the door can be shut against the Huns and the barbarians of the world. Like the comfort of a soft, satin lined coffin . . .

The Choice that Isn't a Choice

But it's her choice, many scream on hearing these things. If a woman chooses to be a mother, who am I to second-guess or criticize. Some will accuse me of not respecting a woman "choice" to become a self-sacrificing mother. "Your generation fought for a woman's right to choose her own future," they will gripe.

Let me simply respond that I'm very suspicious of a "choice" that corresponds exactly to what women have done from time immemorial. A "choice" that exactly matches what a woman has always been expected and required to do. A "choice" that turns out to be exactly what she would have done without the "choice."

What's Wrong With This Picture?

The "apple pie and motherhood" scam robs women of real choices very early on. The question still put to young women is not "Will you have children," but "When will you have children," or "How many children will you have?" Another question always posed to women wavering about motherhood strikes fear with its grim prediction, "Will you regret *not* having children," never "Will you regret having children?"

It is simply a given that women will have babies and that historical expectation has not changed for young women. Indeed, young women appear hell-bent on turning themselves into baby factories. A women's magazine described a group of female MBAs from a top school discussing their post graduation plans. One of them gushed, "I want to have kids right away . . . a big family — four children. Maybe I'll find something to do part-time, but my children will come first." Her decision did not strike her classmates as unusual. Indeed, as other women expressed similar sentiments, everyone nodded in agreement.[88] Hello! You *may* find something to do part-time? This woman just went through a tough program earning an M.B.A., taking up a spot in a top school, a spot that could have educated someone with a commitment to the field. What gives? Do we all have to self-destruct in order to learn anything?

These women are not the exception. A number of studies confirm a retreat to traditional sex roles among well-educated women, or more precisely, a stampede. One study of Yale alumni in 2000 found that among female graduates in their 40s, only 56% were still in the workforce (full or part-time). Another study of Yale female graduates done five years later found the pattern had not changed. A bit over half of the women said work was their primary activity compared to 90% of the men. Another study at Harvard Business School that tracked three classes from the 1980s and 1990s found that only 31% of the women worked outside the home full time and 38% were stay-at-home moms (the rest worked part-time). A 2005 study of female freshman and seniors at Yale, Harvard and the University of Pennsylvania found that 60% said they would stop work or work part-time when they had children.[89] These are the brightest of the bright, and certainly the most privileged.

What about college students and graduates generally? One study surveyed men and women professionals aged 25-35, asking what their top personal concern over the next three years was. For the men, being laid off emerged as the top concern followed by purchasing a home; but fully 50% of the women said their top concern was getting married (presumably a large portion of the other 50% were already married).[90] Consistent with this approach, young women typically do not question women's traditional role as chief caretaker, even when they expect hubby to "help" with household chores.

Equally interesting is the fact that at least 40% of twenty-somethings were raised by divorced or separated parents.[91] Yet a complete disconnect apparently exists between the reality of divorce and how they see their own lives. I can only assume this is, again, a case of "I'm different. It happens to others, but it won't happen to me." Sadly, it can happen to any of us.

What a conundrum! On the one hand, education is certainly not just about job preparation. It's about broadening a person's mind and experiences and expanding their outlook on life. But that gets a tad harder to justify in a professional school which is geared toward a particular career outcome. A dean at Yale College, Peter Salovey, said it best, "What does concern me is that so few students seem to be able to think outside the box; so few students seem able to imagine a life for themselves that isn't constructed along traditional gender roles."[92]

The predictors are there long before college. Ask any high school teacher what drives the overwhelming majority of young women and they'll tell you boys, Prince Charming, getting married, having children. It's not that these young women don't want careers. They do. But they still don't see themselves as the family breadwinner. That's the role of Mr. Right; he will be the prime breadwinner and they see their own careers as something they can take or leave, jump in or out of. College educated women, it would seem, are typically no different.

"What's Wrong With Me? I Don't Have Kids."

The actress Winona Ryder once spoke of wanting to have children despite being single. She confessed to feeling "this weird pressure" to have a child.[93] "Weird," maybe. Unusual, no.

The pressure to have children is so profound that countless women, who for whatever biological reason cannot have children, endure years of painful procedures and expend tens of thousands of dollars in an effort to become pregnant. Or, they seek surrogate mothers, often in foreign countries like India. One woman I knew confessed that she believed she "could not be a real woman" as long as she did not conceive children.

Females grow up expecting to be mothers, even when they don't particularly want to be. I always thought I didn't want to have kids, but that desire translated into the wish to postpone the inevitable. So deep-seated is the conditioning to motherhood in females, that even when young women express a commitment not to have children, the programming is likely to spring up at a later date. Typically this happens when women "settle down" with a partner or approach the "ticking biological clock" of middle age.

The conditioned feeling that she must have a child is so strong in a woman that even those who lead full, meaningful lives, with interesting and satisfying work, typically feel they have missed out on some indispensable life experience. So completely have we been brainwashed about our "true" mission in life, that even women who love their child-free lives, carry the stigma of "emptiness" and "lack of fulfillment" as inescapable baggage.

This is true even for women who cannot and would not spend the daily hours and endless years needed in child-rearing. I meet these women everywhere and the problem is stated something like the following: "I'm happy with what I do; my work gives meaning to my life. I could never give it up, but there must be something wrong with me — I don't have children."

Some women resist the psychological pressure to reproduce and actively choose a childfree life; others are unable to reproduce. Of women up to age 44, 19% are childfree (up from 10% in 1976).[94] Women who choose to be childfree are happy with their choice. Women who find themselves childfree by circumstance rather than choice often carry gnawing doubts about the validity of their lives and the conjured up fear about future regrets. But, as discussed earlier, studies are clear that families without children tend to be happier than those with kids.[95]

The bugaboo about lonely old age without children has also been debunked. The *Journal of Gerontology* reported in 1998 that research shows "no significant differences in loneliness and depression between parents and childless adults. By and large, our children are not there for us in old age. They have, after all, built lives of their own.

Other women succumb to the pressure and have children. I've seen many committed career women, who couldn't see themselves as mothers, give in and have children.

Mildred, a successful business owner, had spoken for years of her misgivings about children in her life. She loved having her own business which she had built from nothing, but felt a lot of pressure from family and friends who kept telling her she was "missing-out." At first the talk made her angry. *She* didn't feel she was missing anything. But, coupled with the messages of a lifetime, Mildred eventually bought into the argument that soon it would be too late. What if she "woke up" one day — as she put it — and regretted her childfree life? Mind you, she didn't regret anything, but she feared that she *might* regret it someday. Interestingly, her husband was indifferent to the idea of children. It was up to her, he said.

After much agonizing, Mildred had a child and was instantly "fulfilled." But she couldn't get back to work soon enough. So Mildred immediately hired a live-in nanny to raise her child. For all intents and purposes, she continued to lead exactly the same life she had lived before her child was born. The child, who is essentially parented by a person other than her mother or father, is there as a testament to the illusion of "fulfillment."

Then there's Aleta St. James who, at age 57, became the oldest woman to have twins. Despite a successful career traveling the world, the pressure to have children persisted. Her friends kept asking when she would do it. In her 50s she told herself, "*I'm not going to live in regret. I really always wanted to have children. I know I'm supposed to bring in children*"[96] [italics mine]. There it is, the double whammy: the mandate (the expectation that women should have children) and the fear (not having children will bring life-long regret).

The Invisible Helping Hand

The scenario is different for most women, of course, who can't afford nannies, live-in or otherwise. Typically, when a career woman has babies, she's on her own. The reality is that, with some notable exceptions, fathers cannot be counted on to share child-rearing in any substantial way. Fathers may "help," but the responsibility still falls to mom. So, having babies triggers an unending cycle of stress and exhaustion while juggling family and job.

The tragedy is compounded by a false sense of motherhood that prevails from earliest childhood. Motherhood, as we know it, means self-denial, self-sacrifice and self-effacement. The traditional definition of motherhood, which still dominates, demands that a woman suppress her own agenda and needs in her child's interests. A mother's own self-fulfillment remains secondary — or nonexistent — in a way that it never does for a child's father. When traditional men, politicians among them, run about extolling the virtues of motherhood and all it entails (self-sacrifice, self-sacrifice and self-sacrifice), one is tempted to say, "Then you do it, if it's so great!" But of course, none of them ever would.

It is not accidental that the United States is almost alone among developed countries for our lack of paid leave for new mothers.[97] We do not make it easy for women to have children. Society says to women, in effect, "We expect you to have children; it's your obligation. But we have no intention of offering support services to make it easy on you (like day-care, health care, paid parental leave). You must bear the full burden of motherhood. And if you think you can 'have it all,' you're crazy. Don't expect any help from us."

The expectation is that work and career should be sacrificed to care for the child. Of course, the essential ingredient in this picture is a well-paid daddy who sticks around for life and who brings home lots of bacon everyday — kind of like the old Hollywood movies where everyone is rich and has dinner in tuxedos. Let's get real!

When poor women are provided with paid health care (Medicaid), food stamps, and other (paltry) support services, they are called moochers, chastised for not earning their own keep, and told to get a job — even though most do have jobs. "If she thinks she can get away with *not* doing it all, she's crazy."

I'll tell you what's crazy. Women having children under these conditions. No social support services. No paid parental leave. No public day-care, quality or otherwise. No equal sharing of the day-to-day menial chores of parenthood by fathers. No wages of their own for mothers who stay home. No social security of their own for mothers who stay home. No pension plans for mothers who stay home. No career support for women who work outside the home and have children. Now *that's* crazy!

The Ultimate Guilt Trip

Women with children who reject the traditional view of motherhood and seek to accommodate their own needs by working full-time outside the home are made to feel something is wrong with them. They are not spending enough time with their children; they are subjecting their children to the dangers of day-care; they are not "there" for their children; they are to blame for whatever ails the child — in short, they are "bad mothers." Putting this burden on women really means that mom should be the personal body servant of her children 24/7, year in and year out. Moms should exist solely for their children. Period. So women suffer destructive self-doubt, guilt and a crisis of identity.

In those rare cases where women don't want children, they are also made to feel selfish and guilty. Women are told from earliest childhood that their role involves accommodating to the needs of others and that means sacrificing their agenda. Pleasing others is how we will be liked and accepted and a large body of research confirms that women want to be liked and accepted above everything else. Not having children, especially for a career, is the ultimate "selfishness," the ultimate failure to please others, the ultimate refusal to "serve." To many, being "my own person" is unforgivable in women.

Who's Sorry Now?

Typically when women have children, they cannot foresee how their lives will change. As young women (and as they approach middle age without children), they are convinced that having a "family" is what they want, only to find, too often, that it is *not* what they want. Life is growth and change, and it's not unusual for women to regret having children, to want a career and a life among adults, where once children seemed enough.

Some years ago, columnist Ann Landers asked her readers to comment on whether they would have children again if they had it to do over. Of the tens of thousands of people who flooded her with responses, fully 70% said they would not choose to become parents again.[98] As Landers reported in an article in *Good Housekeeping*, these negative responses came from a broad cross section of parents, young and old, rich and poor, urban and rural, from all geographical regions of the country. She also noted many letters from parents who claimed their children had ruined their marriages.

When Dr. Phil asked a similar question years later, 40% said they regretted having children. These are not scientific studies, of course, but the outpouring is most interesting. It's surprising to hear how often women express regret, guilt and confusion — anonymously, of course. It is not the sort of thing many women dare state openly. A couple of Dear Abby letters graphically expressed this change of heart and mind.

Dear Abby:

I am currently separated from my husband. We have a 2-year-old daughter — I'll call her "Sherry." We agreed that Sherry should stay a week at his house and then a week at mine. (I live with my mom.) This is working OK for now, but I can't see it working until Sherry is 18.

Here is my dilemma: If I continue to share custody of Sherry, I will always struggle. I have an average job with no college degree, and I really want to pursue schooling and have a career. Also, I have a difficult time emotionally when I have Sherry because she's spoiled rotten and acts like a brat. It stresses me out to be with her. Her father wants full custody, and I'm ashamed to admit that I do not.

People tell me I will regret giving her up, but they don't know how hard it is to go to college and care for a child.

Abby, I am very confused about what to do. I feel like a bad mother for not fighting tooth and nail for full custody like most mothers would.

My husband says it would be no problem for him to have Sherry full time. Should I let him have her? Please respond as soon as possible.

— Feeling Guilty

And another letter:

Dear Abby:

I am a stay-at-home mother who is about ready to explode!

I love my children with all my heart. At one time our first child was very sick, and we went through a lot to adopt our second child. Both experiences made me realize how deeply I love my little ones.

Lately I have completely lost my "thrill" with motherhood and homemaking. If I have to watch "Barney" on TV one more time, wipe one more chin, change one more diaper or dust one more table, I will go berserk! What's wrong with me?

Two other stay-at-home moms in our neighborhood have left their homes and families. Both are now divorced, living in apartments, and the kids are with their fathers. What scares me is that I completely identify with these women.

I have a part-time job three mornings a week while our daughter is in preschool.

I look forward to those mornings. At home I have frequent headaches, but at work I feel great.

I used to have a wide range of interests and a quick wit, but I feel my personality shriveling up and dying while I sweep, do laundry and clean up after the dog.

My family needs me. I have a responsibility to them, which I intend to keep. [But] I'm afraid when I'm through, there won't be any "me" left. What can I do?

—Not OK Kaye

Well, it's tough after the fact. Better to make an informed, careful decision in the first place. For women the questions are profound: Is motherhood for you? Are you allowing for growth and change in your life? What impact will it have on your life and your career if you choose to have children? Are you willing to pay the price of motherhood?

There is no going back.

CHAPTER 4. HEY, WHO AM I?

How Motherhood Limits and Defines Mom as a Person

Helen's Story — and a Question

Jane Tennison in that marvelous series, *Prime Suspect*, was the perfect role for actress Helen Mirren. A gritty, tough, vulnerable and decidedly unglamorous female detective facing sexist discrimination and chauvinism in an all-male department, Jane battled her way up the career ladder, took on her colleagues, chased down the bad guys, spoke her mind, and never turned her back on the lot of them.

In her long acting career Helen Mirren has portrayed every type of woman from the most ordinary to the most exalted. Her role as Queen Elizabeth won her an Academy Award for Best Actress to add to the slew of honors accumulated during a lifetime of brilliant work.

I confess to adoring Dame Helen Mirren, her person and her acting. So when I heard that "60 Minutes" would be interviewing her, I watched. She spoke about her background, her childhood as the daughter of Russian immigrants in England, her work, the roles she played. Her exciting life as an actress began at age 13 in a school play and she has graced stage and screen, directed and produced, and led a fabulously productive and exciting life. In her early sixties at the time of the interview, her career rolled on unabated.

As the intriguing interview ended, Morley Safer looked earnestly at Helen — and there it was. The predictable question. The ubiquitous question. He had to ask it, as if he had heard nothing she said. The question of questions that no man would ever be asked, but no woman can escape . . .

"Aren't you sorry you never had children?"

Without hesitation and very emphatically, Mirren answered, "I'm so *glad* I didn't have children."

"Why?" he asked with a puzzled look on his face.

"Because I've had freedom!"[99]

Crisis of Identity

That motherhood as we know it — self-denial, self-sacrifice and self-effacement — often results in a woman's inability to fulfill her intellect, talents and skills in meaningful work is only part of the problem. It goes beyond damaging or depriving her of "career," financial independence, accomplishments, and recognition in the broader community. It goes beyond suppressing her own agenda and needs in her child's interests. It goes beyond physical and emotional exhaustion. The most terrible part is losing her *self*. Literally.

In every individual life lies a unique core of being — in an existential sense, a mass of infinite possibility out of which we create a distinctive self, a person unlike any other. If being an individual means anything, it means being a unique person. But creating a unique self is difficult. At every turn, conformity rises up to obstruct and dissuade us. The authentic life is one I create for myself. The inauthentic life is one imposed on me by others, defined for me by others. Conformity and sameness, although to some extent an unavoidable part of human existence, are antithetical to individuality. When they completely overtake a life, that person has abdicated responsibility for self.

Motherhood is a category of being that not only imposes definition and demands conformity, its practice requires that a woman's life becomes subordinate to the needs of her child. But to the extent that a person's life is subordinate to the needs of others, dictated by others, constrained by others, in servitude to others, it is not free. To the extent that a person's life is self-directed, unshackled from endless and ongoing obligations to others, able to be and grow, it is free.

Sadly, as things stand, "free mother" is typically an oxymoron.

As if the traditional demands on women to subordinate their lives to children were not enough, an interesting phenomenon has emerged in contemporary motherhood. As discussed earlier, we find among many women, typically middle class women of some means and education, the "intense parenting" trend. These women carry to extremes the subordination of their lives to their children. Every need or imagined need of her child ties these moms to an endless cycle of tending to those necessities, responding to every whimper, keeping the child at arm's reach, reacting to every demand, researching every developmental strategy, taking baby to every play group, photographing every pose — in short, smothering her offspring with continuous, unrelenting attention.

Judith Warner, who writes extensively about motherhood, believes "overinvolved parenting" describes "the mess" so many mothers find themselves in. Again, these women represent the opposite extreme from the neglectful parent. In an ongoing effort to be perfect mothers, they constantly "facilitate" their children like participants in a never-ending seminar filled with activity after activity, with pauses only for sleep. In a grand endeavor to micromanage every moment of their children's lives, countless women wrap their own lives around these little ones, obsessing every step of the way and miring themselves in a cult of trivia. But as women exhaust themselves obsessing over their children's lives, they lose control over their own. They become child-like in an effort to live at their children's level. They no longer exist in an adult world.

Of her own parenting years, Warner says,

> "I was surrounded, it seemed, by women who had surrendered their better selves — and their sanity — to motherhood. Women who pulled all-nighters hand-painting paper plates for a class party. Who obsessed over the most minute details of playground politics. Who — like myself — appeared to be sleep-walking

through life in a state of quiet panic. Some of the mothers appeared to have lost nearly all sense of themselves as adult women."[100]

By any measure, motherhood, with rare exception, embodies a state of subordination to the needs of others. Such a life is decidedly not free in any meaningful sense. Set aside "overinvolved/intense parenting" for a moment, a mother, any mother, must consider the needs of her infant or child in virtually every situation — be that a simple trip to the store (do I take baby, do I leave baby, who will watch baby . . .?), be it work outside the home (can I leave baby for prolonged periods, do I hire a sitter, can I afford daycare, what will I do if baby gets ill . . .?), be it personal development (where do I find time to use my talents and skills, where will the psychic energy come from, can I continue my education and if so, how. . .?), be it time alone for her partner and herself (when do we fit in space and time for each other, do we drop the kids off with relatives, do we hire a sitter, where do we find a reliable sitter, what time must we return to accommodate the sitter . . .), and on and on.

It is simply a fact of motherhood that children are always there, always a big constraint, always needing and demanding service for every aspect of their young, vulnerable lives. The great bulk of a mother's time, thought, emotion, and energy must, of necessity, be directed to her children. (Set aside the question of money for now.) As long as her children need her, every decision in her life, large or small, must take into account her children.

Any honest mother will tell you that when baby enters her life, freedom all but vanishes. It becomes harder and harder to see her life as independent and unfettered, as a unique self in its own right. A mother's identity and her self-worth become inextricably bound up with her children.

The No-Return Policy

It's the ultimate no divorce "marriage," for better or for worse, till death do you part — you and the child. If you have a child and the unforeseen occurs, as it *always* does, you must be prepared to deal with it. It's a package deal with a no-return policy — child and whatever is true of the child — behavioral problems, physical disability, mental illness, sickness, learning disabilities, angst-ridden adolescence, car accidents, criminality, addiction, emotional trauma, financial need, or a host of other problems, large and small. Husbands can be left, parents can be left, siblings can be left, friends can be left. But your child cannot be left — at least not without causing terrible pain to your child, yourself and others who inherit the burden.

We cannot return a child as we do a dress that does not fit. Once a child is born, there is no easy walking away — not for mom, anyway. An enormous personal and social pressure, unlike any other, comes bundled with the package. The child is there, the responsibility is there, and that's it! For life. That has incredible implications for any woman's ability to see herself as an independent and free person, to grow as an individual. Her self-development is constrained at the very least, and her identity obscured behind the mother-child relationship.

If mom walks away to build a life for herself, as some desperate women have done, she is the dreaded "bad mother," worse than a criminal, the lowest of the low.[101] But dads have always been able to walk away from their families without suffering any particular censure. If dad walks, he's still whoever he is — there is no "bad father" stigma comparable to "bad mother." As long as he throws a little money at his children, he's an OK dad.

Who Am I?

Over the years, I have had an extraordinary experience with women in my seminars. I frequently invite women to introduce themselves to the group. Almost without exception, they identify themselves as mothers, despite the fact that such an identification is irrelevant and unhelpful in the professional context we're in.

"I am the mother of two daughters . . ."

"I have a son, Bobby, aged ten and a daughter, Lisa, aged 8 . . ."

"I am a mother and a grandmother . . ."

When I ask them to share their most unique and important accomplishment to date, the fact that they had babies is there, front and center. This despite there being nothing particularly unique about women having children — virtually any woman can do it.

"The most important thing I ever did was have children . . ."

"I guess I'd have to say being a mother . . ."

"Getting pregnant with my daughter is my biggest accomplishment . . ."

It's the rare woman who offers an accomplishment unique to her as an individual.

Even when I ask women to tell the group what they do professionally, in the obvious context of their organization or corporate function, most women feel compelled to announce their motherhood along with their professional job description. Again, in the context, their motherhood, or lack of it, is totally irrelevant — yet there it is.

"I work in Human Resources at X Corporation and I am the mother of three . . ."

"I am Director of Student Affairs at XYZ University and I am raising a daughter, Rebecca who is 11 years old . . ."

"I'm a butcher at M Supermarket and I've got two kids . . ."

So pervasive is the motherhood status response that even childless women feel compelled to announce that fact.

"I work at ABC Agency and I don't have any children . . ."

It's as though somehow it isn't enough to say I do such and such at X Corporation, even in a seminar focusing strictly on workplace issues. It's as though these women have to legitimate their professional jobs by adding that their real function is motherhood. Or is it that women cannot conceptually extricate themselves from motherhood?

Rarely have I encountered a man who introduces himself as a "father" or adds that to his professional identity (as in "I'm an accountant and a father "). They just don't do it.

But it's not surprising that women feel compelled to declare their status as mothers, despite its irrelevance and inappropriateness. Typically, in a woman's mind, she cannot separate motherhood from her identity or from her other functions. What should be her individuality is reduced to a generic function shared by females. "Mother" is who women think they are, so thoroughly have they internalized society's expectation of womanhood.

Then there are the women who cannot articulate any other function in their lives except motherhood. These are typically women who have been out of the workforce for a period, homemakers or "displaced" homemakers.

"I am the mother of Billy and Jane." Period.

Often, to make a point, I will specifically ask women to introduce themselves without any reference to themselves as mothers.

"Tell us about yourself," I ask. "But don't tell us whether you're a mother or not."

Many women sit there dumbfounded, with nothing to say, shrugging and grappling for something to grab hold of. It's an extraordinarily painful, but illuminating, moment. It's as though take away Bobby and Jane and nobody is there. No person, no accomplishment, no purpose — a kind of nothingness where the body of a human being clearly sits. These women look at themselves and cannot see anything if their offspring depart the scene — as, of course, offspring eventually do. They are members of a category, "mother." Take away the category and they don't exist.

It's bad enough that the world does this to women. It's worse that women do it to themselves, measuring their lives in the traditional way a woman is measured — not as a human being responsible for creating her own unique life, her own individual self, but in relation to her children and her role as a mother. And if we're not doing it to ourselves, rest assured there are plenty of women out there who will do it for us. Women like Nora Keller, Elinor Gadon, Susan Patton, Sylvia Ann Hewlett, and so many others.

Keller tells women of her great pleasure at being cocooned in her house with her daughter and positively drools at the "desire, the passionate obsession, to enslave myself to another."[102] She also reveals that her "world shrunk" to the size of her daughter's body after giving birth and that she pulled her daughter from preschool because she could not separate from her.[103] It's beyond embarrassing to hear an adult speak of "enslaving" herself to another, regardless of the age of that other. The damage that does to women who hear this drumbeat of total self-sacrifice again and again is incalculable. Most normal women, might I venture, do not want to picture themselves as "slaves" and can only wonder what's wrong with them that they feel this way.

Women in the matriarchal feminist movement, like Elinor Gadon, also do a number on women with their pop-psychology.

They define women by their ability to give birth and their connection with "Mother Nature." To Gadon, woman as baby-maker (the "Great Mother") is goddess because "women's wombs are their power centers, not just symbolically but in physical fact."[104] Yikes! Human being as a body part!

Taking a different tack, Susan Patton pushes hard for women to marry early because work will wait, but their fertility won't.[105] Hewlett decries the "bad choices" made by top level professional women to remain childfree, the "tragedy" being that they waited too long to have children, let their biological clocks run out on them, missed their chance. So she pressures young women to marry young and have babies right away, quick, quick, hurry, hurry, before it's too late! They can always have careers later (presumably by tucking baby away in a drawer at some point and moving on). If you don't do this, Hewlett warns a generation of young women, you will endure the unspeakable fate of those sad, childless professional women.[106]

Which women, I want to ask? Women like Helen Mirren? Those women doing exciting work, earning top dollar, traveling the world. Those women meeting interesting people, getting exposed to stimulating ideas? Those women known for their imagination and creativity? Those women respected for their expertise and leadership. Those women contributing to their communities . . . ? I know many of these women and not one of them regrets her childfree status (although some regret the lack of a partner). On the contrary, many intentionally chose not to have children.

Every woman (and man) must create her own unique being, however scary and intimidating that may be. None of us wants to be confronted with that terrible question *"Who am I?"* in old age when it's truly too late. How terrible it must be to reach old age with regrets about not doing the things that she wanted and expected to do with her life — to look back and see a hole where once a dream stood.

Not knowing what to do with one's life beyond conforming to somebody else's pre-ordained definition is the ultimate sign of powerlessness. Power is much more than the ability to move others. Power is the ability to move ourselves.

The Building Blocks of the Family

A woman is an individual before she is a mother. People are individuals before they form relationships and have families. It is individuals who are the building blocks of the family and those building blocks form the order of importance in any family. Relationships are secondary and flow from individuals being together. We've made some progress in western cultures with the traditional notion that a woman is defined by her relationship to a man (Mrs. John Smith). Not so with motherhood, where a woman's relationship with her child is primary and she as an individual is secondary or irrelevant.

We have this strange notion that when the female of the family is playing the role of mother well, that is, servicing her children above all else, the family is strong. In fact, all we are doing is raising self-absorbed little people who will grow up believing that they alone are special, that women exist to service others, that mom is not important in her own right but only in relation to them. They, especially if male, may never learn to do necessary, life-demanding chores for themselves. They will carry the notion into school and into the workplace that the menial tasks of life and work belong solely to women.

A world where particular groups of people are preordained to fit the category of servant or slave has long since been discredited — except when it comes to women. Because a woman is not seen as an individual important in her own right, her *self* is subsumed under the family as no other family member is. Her worth exists only in relation to family. In such a circumstance, there can be no *self*-worth, in the strict sense of the word, for a woman.

A Metaphor for the Self-Sacrificial Mom

Judith Warner, in her excellent book, *Perfect Madness*, uses a classic children's story as a metaphor for contemporary motherhood. It's brilliant, so let me repeat the story here.

> A tree loves a little boy and he loves her back. He takes her leaves, climbs her trunk, swings from her branches, eats her apples, and sleeps in her shade. When he grows up, he sells her apples for money, cuts off her branches to build a house, and cuts down her

trunk to make a boat. And then, when he's old and too tired to move, and she's nothing more than a stump, he sits down on her and rests.[107]

It's important for a woman to remind herself that, whatever she decides about having children or not having them, she should not allow herself to be used and used up, to be consumed by her children. That she hold the essential core of her being as inviolate, meaningful and worthy in itself, capable of growth and exploration in the broader world, and hers alone to use as she sees fit. The rules are simple, or should be:

Rule #1: Don't practice self-annihilation via motherhood.

Rule #2: Reread Rule #1.

Rule #3: If you must self-annihilate, there are far easier ways to do it than motherhood.

CHAPTER 5. THE MONEY PIT

The Financial Cost of Having Children

Paying for Love Insurance

Stephanie always wanted to be a mother. She said so whenever she talked about her future.

"I want to have lots of kids," she beamed.

"Earth mother," we called her.

Once I asked why she wanted to have "lots of babies." She looked puzzled by the question and acted as though there must be something wrong with me for asking. After she had sufficiently, and silently, chewed on my stupidity for being so out of it, she replied that babies are what it's all about.

"I adore babies. It's what I want to do," she added emphatically.

"Fine. Just be sure you can support yourself and all those babies," I said, seriously trying to be helpful to a fog-bound young person. Her mother, after all, had "lots of babies," but poppa had left her high and dry with those little ones.

"Yes, but after he left, momma still had us kids," Stephanie retorted. "Without her children, she would have had no one. We love her."

Ahh, as we spoke, the package started to open. A woman's

children can be counted on to stay with her even if poppa takes a leap. I guessed the argument in her mind was running something like this: A woman wants/needs to be loved. A man can't be trusted to keep giving her love. So that's where children come in — a kind of love security blanket. But I'm no dummy. I saw the minefield and backed off real quick.

Still, her response got me thinking about the old adage that women are in love with love. Maybe babies are a kind of insurance policy on love. I remembered reading a woman's account of her reaction to her newborn: ". . . when I sat him up and supported his jaw with my hand, [he] looked rather like a frog with a mass of black hair. I was in love."[108] Strange way to describe it. Not "I loved him instantly," or "What a lovable child," but "I was in love." Falling in love with one's own child? Well . . . The frog thing is weird too — "frog" as in lover boy Prince Charming?

Anyway, Stephanie was one of those women who really did go to college to find a man. As far as we could see, whoever this man turned out to be, his primary purpose would be to produce babies.

By her senior year in college, Stephanie found her man. Adam was younger and he hadn't finished his degree. In fact, he was only a freshman. That wasn't going to deter Stephanie and they married within six months. After the usual princess wedding with the full contingent of bridesmaids and grooms, tuxes and tails — all of which they couldn't afford — they set up house in a small apartment. She took a job — though she never viewed it as more than temporary — and Adam got a part-time job at night while he kept going to school.

Now the reasonable assumption was that Stephanie and her man would keep working for awhile, at least until he could finish his degree. But guess what? Stephanie couldn't wait to have her babies and got pregnant. Ten months after the wedding, an ecstatic Stephanie gave birth to her first child.

After her baby arrived, Stephanie stopped working outside the home. Because that was financially untenable, daddy had to work harder to support the trio — nights and weekends. Money was very tight. It wasn't long before Adam had to drop out of school, take a full-time job (not a well-paying job, since he had no degree). He vowed to finish his studies "somewhere along the way." That all seemed OK by Stephanie, whose next project became buying a home. They were a family now, she argued, and a family needs a proper home. Damn the expense!

To be fair, Stephanie did do some baby-sitting to help with the bills. However, that barely kept the baby in diapers. Somehow, they managed to buy a home — only after Adam took a second job in the evenings. The house was small and had no picket fence or rose-covered trellis, but Stephanie had her dream cottage. So she set about getting pregnant again.

The second baby "broke the camel's back," financially speaking. By the time baby number 2 arrived, Adam had lost his full-time job and was working three part-time jobs. At that point, they had no medical insurance to cover medical expenses. So baby bills began to fill Stephanie's dream cottage. The couple struggled financially as the strain of paying the way for four people exacted its price. But nothing deterred Stephanie. She wanted more children and before long, baby number 3 arrived.

Adam looked gaunt and exhausted as he raced from job to job. He stopped talking about going back to school. Stephanie, meanwhile, reveled in her baby-love, seemingly oblivious to the toll on her husband who had turned into a sperm bank and a money-maker (though not a very good one). To be sure, Stephanie is a great mom.

Before too many years passed, Adam jumped ship and left town after having his second affair. Stephanie is left with the kids and her self-fulfilling prophecy. She has the love of her children.

Paying the Day-to-Day Costs

One woman described her day-to-day financial strains:

> "My husband and I were never well-to-do, but we managed on both our incomes. After the first baby was born, everything changed even though I kept working. The lack of money really started to hurt. Babies always need something. The diapers, formula, clothes, crib, high chair, doctor bills, medicine — there's never an end. We still get by, barely, but it's stressful. There's never any money for the extras that make life more bearable.

By the time our second child was born, we totally stopped going out to dinner or movies. But having no money for entertainment, vacations or luxuries was the least of it. When Tony or I need anything — a new coat, clothes, a better car — there is never enough money. I'd love to visit my sister in Tucson, but that's out of the question. Six months ago, Tony needed to rent a tuxedo and I had to buy a gown to be in his brother's wedding party. On top of that, we had to put together a decent wedding gift. It shouldn't have been a big deal, but we could barely scrape together the money. And last year when the house needed a new roof, we had to take out a loan. That hurt. One more bill to pay every month.

Without the kids, we'd have some money put away for these emergencies. But the kids always need something — clothes, shoes, books for school, lunch money, money for the sports they play or school trips — you can't deny kids what the other kids have. Then there's the doctor bills and medicine. We never indulged them and they've gone without plenty. But it's still hard. And what about college? I don't know how we'll swing that even if the kids work to pay for part of it.

As for saving any money — forget it! Our bank account is barely on life support. I worry a lot about when we get old. Will we ever be able to save enough? I don't want to be poor when I'm old, but the way things look, I'll be living on social security, if that's even around when I retire. I have to hope that when the kids leave home, we'll manage to save a little."

Paying for Mr. Wrong

Judy never imagined herself as a 50% statistic. She believed her marriage would last forever. Sure, she knew people got divorced, but "they" were different. They were the women who got it all wrong — married the wrong man or didn't know how to be a loving wife or didn't care enough about their marriages. Not her — she had married someone special. She was filled with love for Mr. Man and she most assuredly cared about her marriage.

It started so well. Judy went with Alex in college for a couple of years before they married. He played football and could have had any coed he wanted. Women always fawned over handsome Alex and he was something of a ladies' man before they started going steady. But that only made her feel lucky and downright special. After all, Alex rejected all those women and chose her.

After graduation, Judy and Alex had the usual fairy tale wedding in a big church with over 400 guests — generous guests whose combined gifts gave them the down payment for a fine house in the suburbs. Alex joined a top accounting firm with a hefty starting salary (his star status as a football player opened doors). Judy got a job as an assistant in Human Resources at a small corporation earning a salary considerably less than Alex's — three times less to be exact. But that was OK with Judy. Alex made more than enough for both of them.

The early years together were fun. Plenty of money bought whatever they wanted. They got invited out a lot. Alex liked parties and being in a crowd of people. It was all so storybook. Sometimes Judy looked in the mirror and couldn't believe her good fortune.

"You're so lucky," she would whisper to the beaming face in the mirror.

When at last Judy became pregnant, she tried not to make demands on Alex. Even if she didn't feel so hot, she followed him from party to party. In the last months of her pregnancy, when it got too uncomfortable and tiring to move a lot and the baby pressing on her bladder kept her running to the bathroom, Judy stopped going out. That, however, didn't stop Alex.

"Do you mind, honey?" Alex would ask. Well, she did — a little — but she didn't want to cramp his style just because she was pregnant.

Or, "Bob and I really want to watch the football game tonight. Will you be OK?" She thought about the TV they had at home with the same football game, but it wouldn't be any fun for Alex to watch it alone, she thought.

Or, "Some of the guys are getting together tonight. I won't be late." Of course, he often was late, but he was always there in the morning.

He'll settle down when the baby is born, she rationalized. He didn't.

After baby arrived, Judy saw even less of Alex. His excursions got more frequent. The storybook started to tear at the edges. Although she had taken a leave from her job, Judy felt overwhelmed by motherhood and very much alone. Not only was Alex no help, he was seldom around. They started to argue. The quarrels escalated and Alex accused her of being "no fun" anymore.

"You're turning into a nag," he shouted as he stormed out the door.

One morning, after Judy had been up most of night with a crying baby, her husband remarked, "Look at you. You're really letting yourself go."

Then Alex started not coming home all night. Depressed and frantic, Judy told him she couldn't, she wouldn't go on like this. To her shock, he shouted, "Then we won't! I'm out of here."

The separation and divorce were like nothing Judy had ever experienced. It wasn't just the acrimony and the recriminations. It wasn't even finding out that Alex had been seeing another woman for months before they separated. She had begun to suspect as much. The clobbering by economic wind shear hit her hardest.

Suddenly Judy had to worry about money to buy food, money for the mortgage, money for utilities, money for the car insurance, money for all the things her baby needed. That had never happened to her before. She and Alex had saved very little despite Alex's comfortable income, and what they had saved went very quickly. Judy wanted to go back to her job, but who would watch the baby? Her family did not live nearby and she couldn't afford day care on her salary. In desperation, she began babysitting in her home. On weekends, Judy cleaned her neighbor's homes with baby strapped in her port-a-crib while she worked. She borrowed. Still, the heap of bills grew.

Whenever Judy tried to get Alex to pay something toward child support and the house, he would say, "Talk to my lawyer." That got her nowhere. She borrowed money from her family to hire her own lawyer, the cheapest she could find. That pitted her low-priced lawyer against Alex's high-priced lawyer.

The storybook lay in shreds. Judy started peering into the mirror at the desperate face that stared back at her.

"What a fool you've been," she snarled.

Meanwhile the financial battering turned Judy and her family of two into another statistic, a below-the-poverty-line statistic. The months dragged into a year and still no financial settlement from Alex. She couldn't sell the house that was in both their names, and anyway, property values were down. There was hardly any equity built up.

When the shake-out finally came two years later, Judy ended up with a house she couldn't afford (and would only break even by selling) and child-support payments that didn't cover a fraction of the bills her child generated. But it didn't end there. Alex kept missing the payments and Judy kept going to court. Alex had the system tweaked to perfection. Just before the court date, he'd make a payment or two to prove his "good-faith" effort to the court and the process would begin all over.

Had she been alone, without a baby, Judy would have picked up and left it all behind — gone on to build a new life. But there was no walking away with the baby, at least not that she could see.

Deep Pockets

While children are priceless, the cost of raising them is not. The monetary price tag for raising children overwhelms many families. Those costs begin with pregnancy (getting maternity clothes, making a place for baby, buying furniture and baby clothes, paying the medical bills), continue relentlessly until the late teens when a son or daughter either takes a job or goes off to college, and escalate dramatically if college is the option. All too frequently, the price doesn't end with college or a job, but dogs parents for many years or decades as their offspring struggle (or don't struggle!) to built themselves a life. So costly is child-rearing, that *not* doing it has been compared with winning a lottery valued at a quarter of a million to a million dollars.[109]

Estimates for the cost of raising a child vary by income level, geographical location, age of the child and how many children. For a couple or a single parent in the lower income group (income under $59,410), a child will cost on average $9,365 per year for the basics — a total of $159,205 through age 17. In the middle income cohort (income between $59,410 — $102,870) the cost will average $13,305 annually or $226,185 total. Upper income families (income above $102,870) will spend $22,460 per year or $381,820 total.[110]

Now it's important to note that this is a basic, no-frills childhood — without computer, piano lessons, sports equipment and uniforms, summer camp, designer sneakers and clothes, birthday parties, presents, and the like. It does not even include the cost of pregnancy and childbirth or college! Include a few extras and a college education and you're really breaking the bank. A college education alone for a public college averages $13,564 per year; for a private college averages $32,026 a year.[111]

So add college costs and extras to the price tag and you've easily got your quarter million to one million dollar lottery ticket. Mind you, this is all for a single child. Have two or three kids, or more, and the financial sacrifice balloons.

What's more, the loss of income when a woman becomes a stay-at-home mom is *not* calculated at all here. Economists have put the loss for a professional woman who leaves the workforce at roughly one million dollars.[112] Sound impossible? Do a quick calculation: a professional woman earning a modest $45,000 a year (forget raises and benefits) who drops out of the workforce for twenty years will lose a cool $900,000.

In any case, lest you get lost in all these number, focus on the basic point. Raising children is very, very, very expensive! As an aside, it's worth noting that the lower your income, the greater the percentage bite a child will take from the family resources.

The Endless Money Siphon

Too often the financial burden doesn't end after college or when a child finds permanent employment.

Brad's a good kid. He just can't get his act together. He never grew up.

Brad left home at age twenty-two after finishing college. He went to live in another city and married a woman he had dated only one month. After six months, Bard and his wife separated. Distraught, he quit his job and came home to live with his parents. That did not particularly please his mother and father, though they did not see how they could refuse. During that period, they coaxed Brad to get a job and get on with his life so that they could get on with theirs.

After a year of lying about and whining, Brad found a job and eventually moved out. But he needed this and that from his parents. He couldn't afford the deposit on his two bedroom apartment, so could they help — just through this rough spot. Why, they asked, did he really need a two bedroom apartment? He couldn't afford furniture on his salary, so he asked them. They resented Brad's requests, but almost anything seemed preferable to having him back home. So they wrote the checks, even though it hurt them financially.

When Brad got laid off, they helped him again. After all, getting laid off wasn't his fault. What are families for?

Today, his employment history has become a page out of "How Not To Succeed In Business." One moment he "can't stand this job one more minute" and quits. Then he can't find a "real" job. Bills pile up. So he takes part-time jobs, but they don't pay enough. A year after he lands the "real" job, his company downsizes and he's out the door again.

At age forty, he still hits up his parents for money for this, money for that. Either he can't pay the rent this month or he can't meet the car payment or he has no health insurance or the cat needs surgery. Through it all, Brad flits in and out of disastrous relationships. He can't seem to connect with the "right" woman. So dumping the emotional load on mom and dad has become routine.

The mighty grip of the parent trap seems inescapable, try as they might to extricate themselves. The fear haunts them that if they don't help, or if they practice tough love, he will end up homeless. After all, his burdened parents say, "He's our son." The image of the shiny faced little boy who brought them such happiness in his youth is impossible to shake.

Paying for Their Bad Choices

The son of educated parents with every encouragement and opportunity, bright and precocious, Artie brought his parents lots of joy as a child. But along the way he got lost — fell in with a foolish crowd, did some marijuana, started coming home very late at night, and argued frequently with his parents. He resisted going away to a university, began attending a local college and blew off his studies. After a year, he dropped out, took an apartment with his foolish friends and began working at low-paying service jobs. His heartbroken parents could only watch his stupid choices from afar.

Marriage to a very young air-head slid quickly into divorce, an entirely predictable outcome. In an effort to "save" their son, his parents financed a small business venture with their hard-earned money. Artie lasted in business for barely a year. A second marriage followed and although Artie settled down and began raising a family, his bad choices followed him relentlessly — the financial consequences of low paying jobs and mounting debts. Artie's bad decisions also dogged his parents who years later still find themselves picking up the financial pieces — in the interest of their grandchildren, they rationalize.

"It's *my* life" is the constant refrain from young people who resent their parents' perceived "interference." It's predicated on the idea that mom and dad should not interfere because their grown children are responsible for themselves and they will live with the outcome of their choices. These same children, of course, think nothing of appearing on mom and dad's doorstep for help, especially financial help, when their bad choices go wrong. Then, it seems, their lives are their parents'.

What Not Having It All Really Means

When women are told they cannot have it all, money looms as a big, if hidden, piece of the "all." For a family of modest means, the additional demands on their pocketbook for having babies can be devastating. Even a comfortable middle class family will have to make financial sacrifices. This lack of enough money undermines a sense of security about the present and causes anxiety about the future.

But folks are expected to content themselves with less because, as the saying goes, "Money doesn't buy happiness," a saying no doubt concocted by the rich to soothe the longings of the poor who might aspire to their wealth. If money can't buy happiness, it can buy everything else. One thing is clear. The lack of money sure can buy a lot of unhappiness.

One of the best ways for most people, especially women, to ensure financial distress or money shortages is to have a baby or two or three. This distress may be lessened by the presence of an employed father or partner. True. But let's review again a few messy facts. The divorce rate is 50% overall (higher for young people), so the odds that daddy will stay in the picture permanently are at best 50-50. Upon divorce, most women will not receive alimony. Even if they get child support, it will be inadequate by far, often sporadic, and typically secured after a nightmarish ordeal. Women who left the workforce or downsized to a part-time or lower paying job will be especially vulnerable.

The picture for families headed by women is not pretty. Fifty-eight percent of families headed by working women are low-income.[113] These working women hold jobs in retail, food service, healthcare, and the like that typically offer few benefits or opportunities.

All told, it's estimated that 80% to 90% of all women will be solely responsible for their finances at some point in the lives (because they never married or formed a long term relationship, or they separated, divorced, became widowed, etc.).[114] If this happens with children in the picture, the results can be disastrous.

The stark reality is that, short of being independently wealthy or earning a good salary, mothers in the United States have almost no financial safety net if daddy splits. It would do well for women to remember this instead of daydreaming about Prince Charming fairy tales. Better yet, remember he rides a white horse and can leave as quickly as he came.

CHAPTER 6. GODZILLA MOM

When Motherhood Harms the Child

The Police Blotter

The headline sprawled across the front page: "Toddler's Death Brings Shock: Words Can't Begin to Describe It." Police found the body of little Imani Jennings, 20 months old, in the squalid apartment she shared with her 18-year-old mother and her mother's 15-year-old-boyfriend. The child died of "multiple blunt force trauma," the cold police report read. The horrible reality: She died at the hands of the boyfriend who used his fists, a metal rod, cable cords and metal bedsprings to beat the toddler because she urinated on the floor. Police have established that little Imani suffered routine beatings during her short life from both her mother and the boyfriend.[115]

Just three pages in, another headline slaps the reader: "Police Accuse Mother of Branding Daughter." Tammy Smith stands charged with five counts of child abuse and assault of her six year old daughter. She burned the word "wimp" into the child's neck.[116]

It's hardly possible anymore to read a newspaper that doesn't carry a story of child abuse. But only the worse cases make it to the media. It's not always such horrific physical abuse. Often it involves psychological abuse or neglect. But it happens again and again.

There was a time when even the worst cases were not so public. Child abuse, considered a "family" matter, was almost every community's dirty little secret, hidden from sight, forgotten or ignored, except for the most egregious cases. That has changed to some extent, but we have not begun to adequately address the problem. For me, a horrible awareness of the rampant child abuse crisis started years ago with the story of little Elisa.

A City Story

Her photograph splashed across the nightly news and the cover of *TIME* magazine, tearing at the hearts of strangers around the country. Elisa Izquierdo, 6 years old, whose battered and sexually abused body was found on the eve of Thanksgiving, became the symbol of child abuse for a generation. She had apparently died at the hands of her mother, Awilda Lopez, who later confessed to murdering her child.[117]

Elisa's story screams to be told again and again for the lessons it teaches us. A crack addict when Elisa was born, Ms. Lopez had been accused of neglecting her other children, a son and daughter, both of whom had been taken from her just a month before Elisa's birth. Born with cocaine in her blood, Elisa went to live with her father, who apparently cared for her and provided a loving home despite limited means. After Ms. Lopez completed drug treatment and her children were returned to her, Elisa was allowed to visit her mother on weekends. But those visits ended when her father and teachers noticed bruises, scratches and emotional distress on her return.

By all accounts, Elisa's brief time with her father was happy except for her weekends with her mother. A "beautiful, radiant child," people said of her. In fact, for awhile, Elisa experienced some very good fortune. Her father enrolled her in a Montessori day school and when he could not meet the tuition payments, Prince Michael of Greece, a benefactor of the school, began sponsoring Elisa, so taken was he by the exuberant child. The Prince pledged to finance Elisa's education in a private school through graduation from high school.

But little Elisa's happiness was short lived. When her father fell ill and died, Elisa went to live with her mother, who inexplicably pulled her out of preschool and away from her good fortune. Ms. Lopez did not have to take the child. A cousin of Elisa's dead father went to court seeking custody of Elisa out of fear for her safety. But Elisa's mother would not grant her custody and her history of child neglect did nothing to deter authorities.

So began a year and a half of torture, apparently at the hands of her mother. Elisa became withdrawn and appeared with bruises, scars, limps, balding hair, abnormally frequent urination and other signs of physical and sexual abuse. At one point, she suffered a severe and painful shoulder fracture that went untreated for three days.

Signs of a deeply disturbed child grew more intense as little Elisa began hallucinating. Her behavior screamed for help. Elisa began setting fires, rubbing feces on the refrigerator, hiding her soiled underwear in a hole under her bed, and defecating and urinating in her bed. One neighbor later told of hearing Elisa pleading, "Mommy, please stop, please stop," through the thin walls of her apartment. Her mother, as it turned out, made her eat her own feces, locked her in a closet, beat her, used her head to mop the floor, and sexually violated her with toothbrushes and hairbrushes.

Despite attempted interventions by social workers, school administrators and teachers, Elisa inexplicably remained with her mother, until her twisted corpse was discovered by police. Little Elisa had been beaten to death.

In the much publicized case of Elisa Izquierdo, news media probed what they saw as the central question surrounding the abuse and murder of the child: How had the "system" failed to save Elisa? That is certainly a central question. The Child Welfare Administration responsible for Elisa's case, and the politicians who stripped it of its ability to do its job through budget cuts, deserved all the sanctions heaped on them.

But a more important question needs to be asked: Why was this child born and why was she allowed to stay with her mother, given the horrific circumstances? If we must point fingers at the "system," we need to ask why it is at pains to insure that people meet minimum requirements to drive a car, operate a restaurant, hunt and fish, work as plumbers, but has no minimum requirements to bring a human life into the world, much less provide minimum standards of care for that human being. How can someone like Awilda Lopez bring a child into this world? Ms. Lopez was so obviously incompetent (physically and emotionally) to have children, so obviously disturbed and in desperate need of help herself. A crack addict, she conceived Elisa in a brief encounter in a homeless shelter with a man who worked there, at a time when she could not care for the two children she already had. And by the time Ms. Lopez was arrested at age twenty-nine for the murder of her daughter, she had borne a total of six children.

Elisa did not ask to be born. Worse, given the choice of whether to be born into the life she endured or not, Elisa surely would have declined. But Elisa did not have that choice. It is reasonable to conclude that given the prolonged fear, pain and torture — physical and emotional — this child suffered, no life would have been preferable. Yet her conception and birth were almost certainly unthinking and unplanned. To put the best face on it, Ms. Lopez probably conceived Elisa in a moment of escape that offered solace and relief from the pain of her own life. A new human life was the unfortunate by-product of that moment.

Why use Elisa as a case in point? Surely this is an extreme example of a child who, by every rational standard, should never have been born. Measured against a Norman Rockwell image of the family, Elisa's story is extreme. But unfortunately, countless children here and around the world suffer indignities, deprivation, and abuse quietly, day in and day out, their stories never reaching beyond the walls that confine them. No media news report tells the pain of their particular lives. Sadly, while extreme, Eliza's story is not unique.

In the United States alone, roughly 3.3 million reports of child abuse involving 6 million children reach authorities each year. But, according to state and local child protective services, most cases are never reported and it's estimated that 20% of children in the United States experience some form of abuse.[118] Most people who witness or know of child abuse, two out three, admit they did not report it to authorities. Officially, five children a day (1,825 a year) die as a result of abuse and neglect in the United States, although, again, it's estimated that the real

number is higher — at least twice as high.[119] Most child fatali-
ties due to abuse are not recorded as such on death certificates.

Child abuse occurs at every socioeconomic level, across cultural and ethnic lines, in all religions, and at all educational levels.[120] One in four children lives in a household with an alcoholic
adult, a major cause of abuse.[121] Estimates of sexual abuse in girls
range from 20% to 25% of all girls, while 5% of boys are sexually
abused, overwhelmingly by family members.[122]

No, Elisa's case is shocking only because we saw it in plain
view and because it came to the ultimate bad public end —
murder. We all know such children — the "ragamuffins" of the
world — unloved, uncared-for, badly treated. Many of us have
been those children and we carry the psychic and physical scars
to prove it.

A Suburban Story

Susan, a full-time homemaker, had five children, one after the
other. She lived in a fine house in a good neighborhood. Every
morning her husband went off to work, briefcase in hand, and
Susan was left to care for the children until he returned home
late in the evening. Neighbors saw little of Susan, who kept to
herself in her fine house. The children, however, were everywhere to be found.

A routine established itself. After her husband left, Susan
dressed and fed the children breakfast. Then she sent them outside and locked the door. She and the house were off limits to
her children for the whole day, except for a brief lunch-time
when they were fed and put out to play again. If they missed
that lunch window of opportunity when their mother opened
the door briefly, they missed lunch. Only an emergency — a cut
head, a bad fall, a neighbor banging on the door with a wounded
child in tow — unlocked mommy to the crying youngster.

I remember the first time I became aware of the locked door,
shortly after the family moved into the neighborhood during
summer. Little Cindy, Susan's four-year-old, knocked on my
door and asked to use our bathroom. I was puzzled since the
child lived right next door.

"I can't go there. Mommy keeps the door locked," Cindy said.
"I can't bother her."

The children seemed "normal" enough as they played with my son and the other neighborhood children. They had everything they needed of a material nature, a fine house, nice clothes, food. But these small children (aged three and up) were too young to be left to their own devices, all day, day after day, roaming the neighborhood, crossing streets at will, hanging about the homes of others, craving attention. What hidden scars they bore from the clear and unrelenting message that mommy wanted them away from her as much as possible and daddy was largely absent couldn't be seen.

What psychic pain Susan herself suffered wasn't clear either. Was she unable to cope with five children? Did she crave to be alone? Was she laboring year after year on some hidden work, some great masterpiece? But one question is clear, even if the answer is not. Why have children — and keep having them?

A Small Town Story

Angie, on the other hand, did not live in a fine house and her husband did not go off every morning with briefcase in hand. He was a drunk. To call him an alcoholic would put too nice a face on it. Matt was a fall-down drunk, plain and simple. He "lived" in dingy bars and earned his booze by cooking for the guys, cleaning, or whatever. As for paid labor, Matt worked only sporadically at odd jobs, although Angie seldom saw any of that pittance. He periodically impregnated Angie and did not provide for his family. If his bragging was to be believed, he had children by other women as well. Certainly, he was known to go off with women other than his wife, once for two years. Despite whatever pain she may have felt, Angie kept taking Matt back. And she kept getting pregnant, six times in all. Once she miscarried and after the birth of her last child in her 40s, Angie was so distraught, she nearly had a breakdown.

Through it all, Angie and her children lived — not very well — on public assistance. Her tiny walk-up apartment consisted of basically three rooms, a kitchen and two bedrooms, plus a bathroom and a small pantry-like space off the kitchen. In the kitchen was an old kerosene stove that offered the apartment's only heat and had to be filled by hand with kerosene lugged up the stairs from an outdoor shed. The only furniture to speak of in the kitchen was a large, old, painted wooden table with wooden chairs sitting in the middle of the room which served as the family's living room. The two bedrooms, one behind the other, slept the whole family. The farthest bedroom — windowless — never felt the warmth of the stove on bitterly cold winter nights or the coolness of a breeze on sweltering summer days. The bathroom had only a tub and toilet, no sink. The pantry space off the kitchen barely accommodated a small cot where, in later years, Matt crashed after his drunken binges.

Angie and Matt's children endured a hard life, to put it mildly. One son's most vivid memory of childhood is dragging poppa out of loud, seedy, dimly lit saloons, day and night. When Matt got into his drunken states, someone in the bar would call home to ask the family to come take him away. Matt's son describes pulling his father along the streets, picking him up when he fell, dragging him up the stairs to their apartment. He vividly recalls the time Matt fell down a flight of steps and lay in a heap in a pool of blood, and the time Matt passed out on the sidewalk and one of his drunken pals knelt over him shouting, "Matt, don't die!" over and over. Each time his son, terrified, ran for help. A big burden for a little boy.

On those occasions when Matt managed to drag himself home, the kids lay in bed late at night, listening to pop banging around the kitchen, cooking up a storm. Often drunk, pop would fall asleep or collapse in the middle of his stove-top venture, leaving the gas flame on and the pans boiling to a crisp. Matt's children describe the fear they suffered in those days — of fire and gas, of food burning on the stove unattended, of pots boiling over and extinguishing the flames, leaving the silent killer seeping from the burner. One of them would creep into the kitchen after the banging subsided to "check the gases." And because Matt was a heavy smoker, they had to check for burning cigarettes left to torch the place at will. How many times they saved their own lives, no one can remember.

Poverty took its toll, too. Hunger stalked the family, especially at the end of the month when money and food ran out. And the little things hurt — watching other kids eating an ice cream cone on a hot summer day and not having any, seeing other kids going places with their dads and having no dad to take them anyplace, sitting on the tenement stoop and watching a kid ride by on a shiny new bike . . . The poverty drove them all to take odd jobs at a very early age, before their teens had even begun.

But worst of all was Matt's indifference to the children he fathered. They floated about on the far periphery of his life, as insubstantial as clouds — no concern of his. Matt came and went as though his children didn't exist. He was never there, not for birthdays, not for holidays, not when they were ill, not when they graduated. He was invisible in their good and bad times, but in their faces in his bad times. He brought them no joy, no emotional attachment, no caring, no provisions, no support, no moral guidance. He did bring them fear, anxiety, anger and the violence of the drunk, leaving them emotionally needy for life. And he stole from them a childhood of innocence, security, peace and love.

And what of Angie? A good woman, a simple woman, an uneducated women, she did her best for her children. But what was she thinking when she had children with Matt the drunk, Matt the non-provider, Matt the disappearing act? Not the children, that is clear.

I've known so many women like Angie, popping out babies while in bad relationships. Their children pay the terrible price of their mother's — what? — dependency, ignorance, self-absorption, victimization, powerlessness . . . ?

A Television Story

I was channel surfing on television. One of the many trash talk shows caught my eye because the topic was emblazoned across the screen: "Women who deliberately get pregnant." I watched in horror as the father in the case of the "woman who deliberately got pregnant" emerged on stage — with his mother. A short, slight boy with a crumpled tee shirt, baggy jeans and scuffed sneakers hunched down in a chair on stage, his legs sprawled in front of him. Barely sixteen, Bobby kept one finger in his mouth, sucking or chewing his nail as he mumbled mostly incoherent answers to the host's questions. He looked like a sullen little kid in grade school. It seems Bobby was having sex with Jodie but was not thinking of having children. He didn't want children, he said, but Jodie went ahead and deliberately got pregnant. Bobby was surprised and mad when he found out Jodie was pregnant. The conversation went something like this:

"Did you take precautions not to have children?" the host asked.

"Naw," the boy responded.

"Why not?" the host asked.

With a shoulder shrug, the tee shirt muttered, "Dunno. Never thought about it."

The host, feigning incredulity, asked the boy if he knew how babies were made.

Indignant, the boy retorted, "Yeah, sure."

"Then how can you say you were surprised to find out that Jodie was pregnant?" the host persisted.

Another shrug. Mumble, mumble.

When Jodie appeared on stage with her mother, things got no better. She sat up in her chair with a grin across her carefully made-up face. When asked if she wanted to have a baby, Jodie tossed her curly hair, each ringlet looking like it had been pasted in place.

"Sure. I guess so. I mean, why not?" The grin got wider and sillier.

"But you're only sixteen," the host pressed.

A nod, another grin.

"Why did you want to have a child?"

Another shrug followed by, "I don't know." Another silly grin.

"Did you think of terminating the pregnancy at any point?"

Puzzled look. "No." Shrug. "I mean, like . . . what for?"

"What do you want to do now?" the host asked.

"I don't know." Shrug, head toss. "I guess, like, I guess I want to live with Bobby." the grin said. "Like, you know . . ."

To make a bad story short, Jodie had had the baby, had no idea why she had the baby, couldn't provide for it (on *any* level), wanted to live with the tee shirt, but lived with her mother (who didn't seem to have much more upstairs than her daughter). Yet what struck me most about the show was not the rank stupidity of Bobby and Jodie. It was the fact that neither the host nor anyone in the audience talked *about the baby*. It was all Bobby and Jodie and why and what and how. Would they marry? Did they really love each other? Were they ready for children? How would their lives change if they moved in together? Was Jodie's mother prepared to give up her daughter? . . .

No one asked, "Do you think it's good for this child to be born to two kids? What will happen to this child? What kind of life will this child endure? Did you ever give a moment's thought to the child?"

Nobody said, "This scenario is *not* good for the baby."

A Jet-Set Story

Fran was another case in point. She grew up in a family of wealth. Her millionaire father ran an inherited family business when he wasn't skiing in Switzerland or hobnobbing with the "rich and famous" on the French Riviera. Fran's mother was, as the newspapers referred to her, "a socialite." When I met Fran at a college event I spoke at, she was a freshman. I remember being struck immediately by the sad look on her face. She seemed unable to smile, even when everyone around her was laughing and having a good time. I sat next to Fran at a dinner the young women hosted for the event. Through most of the meal Fran seemed shy and very reserved. I tried to draw her out, to ask about her college major, her interests, anything that would get her talking. Nothing elicited more than a few words until somehow her parents crept into the conversation. Then a torrent flowed. Before she had finished, I wanted to cry for her.

Here was this well-dressed rich kid in a very expensive college getting the best education money could buy, but her unhappiness was visible from every pore. By the time she was through unloading, I had pieced together the following profile of her life: Her parents gave her everything she wanted. She had her own sports car, all the clothes she could wear and more, vacations . . . The one thing she didn't have was parents, in any real sense. They gave her no love, no emotional support, no guidance. Fran was raised by a stern nanny from infancy and endured long separations from her parents as a child. She grew up on a sprawling estate very much alone, except for the servants. When she was very young, she was sent to boarding school where she didn't see her parents for months at a time. When she did see them, they were busy or distant or entertaining friends. During holidays, her parents went abroad a great deal, so Fran spent her vacations from school with friends or relatives or alone at the estate. Her parents did not take her with them when they traveled.

"You wouldn't enjoy it," they told her, or, "It's not a place for a child."

Fran looked at me with the most vulnerable, sad look I think I've ever seen.

"I got so depressed one Christmas," she told me, "I tried to kill myself. But I couldn't even do that right."

When she said that, I had a sinking feeling in the pit of my stomach. She was 14 at the time of the suicide attempt and full of self-loathing. Her story, as she told it, sounded like some rich girl–poor girl cliché or a bad soap opera.

"My analyst thinks I should get a life," she added. "But I get depressed a lot." She paused for a long while, then asked, "Why do people have kids, anyway?"

Why, indeed.

About nine months after dinner with Fran, I met the Dean of Students from her college. I asked about Fran.

"Is she well?"

A frown broke the Dean's forehead. "I'm afraid not. She killed herself two months ago."

To impose life on a human being is very serious business. It is a profoundly moral issue and there are times when having a child — the "pro-life" folks notwithstanding — is immoral. The fact that we have the biological equipment to have babies is not enough to justify having babies. What quality of life that child will endure at my hands is the most basic of all questions in the decision to have a child. Yet few people seem to ask it.

A Homeless Story

Melissa is known as a "throw-away" or a "couch kid" — a child who has been cast out by her family and who moves back and forth from the streets to the couch of a friend or anyone who will take her in for a few nights. Dressed in old and tattered clothes, 16-year-old Melissa survives as best she can alone on the streets, depending on the kindness of friends and strangers who periodically make a temporary place for her on a couch or mattress.

After her mother turned her out, Melissa went to the streets. A tough girl who asserts there's nothing wrong with her life, reflects in her face a different reality. When she was only one year old, her mother was arrested on charges of endangering the welfare of her child by leaving Melissa with someone who injured her. After that, the infant Melissa went to live in a foster home until her grandparents took her in. When they moved away, Melissa went back to live with her mother, who in the interim had also had her two sons taken away on charges of endangering their welfare. Eventually, Melissa's mom threw her out, complaining that her daughter refused to obey the "house rules."

So Melissa moves about the streets in an aimless existence. She has dropped out of school, not surprisingly, and when asked what she will do, she shrugs and responds that she doesn't know. She does know that she hates her mother for failing to love and care for her, and she is angry a lot. In an unguarded moment, Melissa confesses the awful truth about her life, "At times I want to cry. I don't let people see me cry . . . . I want to start my life over."[123] Yes, if only she could.

Melissa's story is depressing in itself. But more horrifying is the fact that she is not alone — not by a long shot. The director of the local residential services of a nonprofit agency that has dealt with Melissa estimates that 500 teenagers like Melissa contacted her agency last year alone. That's 500 children in one year in a not very big city.[124] Since there is no reason to believe that our city is any worse or any better than other cities, the number of young people suffering in this way nationally must be large. The rest of us can only imagine the miserable lives these "throw-away children" endure.

A Tabloid Story

The infamous case of Lisa Steinberg raises many relevant issues.[125] In 1987, six-year-old Lisa was beaten to death in her home. Although Joel Steinberg and Hedda Nussbaum were not her birth parents and had gotten Lisa illegally as an infant, she lived as their daughter under their care.

By every account Joel brutally battered Hedda throughout their twelve year relationship. When Lisa's body was found and her parents arrested, Hedda appeared with her face so battered, she was barely recognizable. Indeed, women's organizations rushed to Hedda's defense and likened her to a concentration camp victim, unable to leave Joel, her captor. Soon, what was Lisa's story became Hedda's story.

Yet Hedda was no ordinary "victim." Well educated with a long career as a children's book editor, Hedda lived in a sado-masochistic relationship where cocaine use was routine. She repeatedly turned down offers of help from people who knew about her battering — doctors, colleagues and others. Hedda and Joel were apparently consenting adults in a bizarre, long-term relationship.

But little Lisa did not consent and was truly the victim. Her destruction did not happen overnight, nor was her final beating an isolated incident. Lisa endured many well documented atrocities.[126]

While she did not give birth to Lisa, what, in fact, was Hedda responsibility to Lisa, whom she took into her home as a daughter? That is, what is a mother's responsibility to her child? In no way does this question absolve Lisa's father — he was a brutal monster long before Lisa entered the picture and he went to prison for his crime. Hedda, on the other hand, was convicted of no crime.

Let us assume, as most do, that Hedda played no direct role in the ongoing abuse of Lisa. The crux of the issue lies in the fact that Hedda allowed the infant Lisa to become part of her violent household and to remain in that household, as indeed she did to a second child, a boy, who managed to escape the pair with his life.

By extension, we may ask about any mother who brings a child, through pregnancy or adoption, into a home with a violent partner or for that matter into any home where the potential for abuse and neglect is real. Nearly 30% of all women are victims of domestic violence[127] (some put the figure higher). This violence, in turn, has serious negative consequences for their children's long term behavioral, emotional, social and cognitive development. Males are more likely to become abusers themselves and females are more likely to be abused themselves later in life.[128]

What are we to conclude about becoming a mother in such circumstances? What should we think of the battered woman who remains with her batterer and, worse, keeps a child in that setting? She certainly has a "right," strange as that may be, to stay with her batterer whether out of choice, fear, financial need or whatever reason. But does she have the right to inflict that day-to-day existence on a helpless child? What of the woman who knows of her own propensity for neglect or violence and has a child? To conclude that motherhood in such instances is ignorant puts the best face on it. Motherhood in such circumstances is difficult, if not impossible, to justify on any criteria, personal, social or moral. (None of which is meant to excuse her partner in any sense.)

Dirty Little Secrets

As a people, we have a need to deny the atrocities and indignities that the children among us endure. Sometimes parents in the families where these outrages occur suffer this same denial. Sure, we watch television talk shows that "expose" the problem of child abuse in its many forms — and we are horrified. But we are horrified as voyeurs watching some seedy drama that happens "out there," somewhere. When it comes to our own homes, neighborhood, and community, we turn away from any hint of these outrages. "I was so shocked it could happen *here!*" is a frequent refrain among neighbors when a case of child abuse comes to light in their community.

Offenses against children range from incest to sexual abuse, from physical battery to psychological torment, from neglect to oppression. They are the dirty little secrets children know but cannot talk about or protect themselves against.

Again, we are not talking about a few children here and there, but an estimated 20% of children. Between four and seven children die every day of abuse and neglect in the United States, which has the worst record among industrialized nations.[129] These cases of child abuse typically do not include the intangible abuses of the spirit and mind that take the form of repeated verbal lashings. Nor do they include the children of battered women who, while not physically abused themselves, must suffer the terror of watching their mothers beaten again and again. No, the problem is not an isolated one "out there," somewhere.

Every abused child has, or had, a mother and a father, at least at conception — the people directly responsible for that child's birth and care. It is their responsibility to protect that child from abusive atrocities. But sadly, we know that in the majority of abuse and neglect cases, one or the other (or both) of these parents is the abuser.[130]

The long term impact of abuse on children, and its resulting emotional chaos, is well documented. Fully 80% of young adults abused as children meet the criterion for at least one psychiatric disorder at age 21.[131] Survivors carry their wounds into adulthood, often experiencing chronic depression or anxiety, post-traumatic stress disorder, eating disorders, low self-esteem, suicidal thoughts, difficulty trusting others and problems with sexual intimacy. Nearly two-thirds of people in treatment for drug abuse were abused as children.[132]

The repressed trauma of abuse victims can even affect workplace relationships where family dynamics and family issues are often played out. Survivors carry around a great deal of emotional baggage, not the least of which is intense anger that can be triggered in a way disproportionate to a particular event. Often survivors are underachievers on the job because the abuse has eroded their self-esteem, or they may act as overachievers who set impossible standards for themselves in a vain effort to prove their adequacy to the world.

The tragedy of abuse reflects a terrible cycle of pain. An unusually large percentage of criminals in prison suffered abuse as children since abused children are nine times more likely to be involved in criminal activity in their lifetime.[133] People who abuse others often come from families where they themselves were abused. One out of three abused children will go on to abuse their own children.[134] Sexually abused girls are 25% more likely to become pregnant as teens and are more likely to engage in risky sexual behavior, putting them at greater risk to contract STDs.[135]

So where does the problem begin and where does it end? We come back to the question of having the child in the first place and whether we can justify that birth. Likewise, in cases of adoption, foster care, or guardianship, can we justify bringing that child into a situation that can potentially inflict serious harm on him or her? Like it or not, women overwhelmingly bear the responsibility of rearing their children, so they must ask if they are psychically able to provide for the child's physical, emotional, and moral well-being.

Going It Alone

In the how-can-we-harm-our-children (not to mention ourselves) department, single motherhood ranks way up there, with some notable exceptions. Single motherhood is increasing and the outlook for most of these children is not pretty. Fully 41% of births in America are to single women, a number that has increased steadily for decades (only 6% in 1960).[136] The younger a mother is, the more likely she is to be single. Among all young women, 3 out of 10 will become pregnant at least once during their teen years and the overwhelming majority are not married or in a committed relationship.[137] Of course, not all pregnancies result in a birth and the teen pregnancy rate is dropping.

Having children in these circumstances does *not* appear motivated by a desire to give a child a wonderful life. Because the vast majority of teen pregnancies are to single teens and a staggering 82% of these teen out-of-wedlock pregnancies are unplanned,[138] we find unwanted children being brought into extremely difficult circumstances. Even in those cases where the birth is planned, we hear a litany of selfish reasons that have nothing to do with the well-being of the child: "I need someone to love me," (Hello? It's the *baby's* obligation to love *you*?) "I don't want to 'miss out' on being a mother," (You think maybe waiting a few years to say this might make sense?), "I thought the baby's father would marry me if I had his baby" (Never mind that overwhelmingly these fathers abandon the pregnant girl.).

Can these children expect a decent life? Sadly, these children will suffer economically, physically, emotionally, socially, and in other ways. The economic deprivation is easiest to document. Children born to single mothers suffer disproportionately from poverty. Fully 70% of children in single mother families are poor or low income as compared to only 32% of children in other types of families.[139]

Yet poverty does not begin to touch the host of problems children born to single moms typically experience. They are more likely to be low birth weight babies (a consequence of poverty and lack of prenatal care) and therefore more likely to suffer from birth defects as well as other physical and mental illnesses. These children are more likely to experience behavioral and academic problems than children in two parent families, more likely to be crack babies or suffer from fetal alcohol syndrome, more likely to drop out of high school themselves, more likely to be raised by someone other than their parents (grandparents, relatives, foster parents), more likely to end up in the juvenile justice system, more likely to be poor as adults, more likely to become unwed teen mothers if they are girls, and more likely to become incarcerated, unemployed and uninvolved with their own children as adults. It's not a pretty picture.

That's My Baby!

Too often, the "decision" to have a child does not include any consideration of the child and the life that child is likely to endure. Too often, the child is merely an instrument of someone else's purposes. The need to be loved. The need for someone to love. The expectation that a child will fill a void in an adult's life. The desire to "have a family."

Having a baby can result from the wish to fulfill oneself — the desire to "round out" one's life, to experience as much of life as possible or to accomplish some perceived mission in life, religious or otherwise. Or the child is a result of a couple's desire to "express" their love for each other. Sometimes we use a child to cement a shaky relationship on the expectation that a child will shore up a disintegrating partnership and keep a mate from leaving. Other times pregnancy becomes a "trick" to get the father to commit to marriage.

Then there's the desire to perpetuate oneself, to "pass on the family name" and/or to have heirs. A man may need to display his virility to the world — a kind of macho impulse to "prove" his manhood by impregnating a woman. Conversely, a woman feels the need to establish her femininity, that is, she needs to legitimate her life in the eyes of the world by fulfilling her "true" mission in life as a mother.

Sometimes we long to escape from a boring, stressful or oppressive job and what better legitimates that impulse than motherhood. Other times we want to please someone else. So we have a child to satisfy a mate who wants offspring or to provide our parents with grandchildren or to give an only child a brother or sister to play with.

Or we want a personal assistant. The child will care for us in old age or tend to our needs in illness or periods of want.

And one that beats them all. In a "Dear Abby" letter, a woman having problems in her relationship wrote, "I am considering getting pregnant 'accidentally' so that even if we got divorced, I'd have some child support coming in."[140]

These and the many other self-centered reasons why people have children are not, in themselves, justification for imposing life. Each and all of them ignore the well-being of the child or, at the very least, make it secondary to our personal desires and needs.

Unplanned Parenthood

In the worst case scenario, no "decision" to have a child occurs at all and children emerge as unplanned and unwanted consequences of sex. Far from unusual, unplanned pregnancies litter the landscape in all segments of society. Roughly one-half of all pregnancies in the United States are unplanned.[141] Again, this figure is much higher among teens, whose pregnancies are unplanned 82% of the time.[142] Of those pregnancies brought to term, the consequences for these unplanned, often unwanted children can be disastrous.

Sometimes a woman will have a number of unplanned pregnancies. Recently I read with dismay a newspaper story of a woman who experienced six unplanned pregnancies. Six! A prostitute and drug addict who went from arrest to arrest, from rehab to rehab, this woman essentially abandoned her children, only four of whom survived. Without a mother or father, these crack babies were consigned to different foster homes and the transient life of insecurity and emotional deprivation that often entails. None will ever know their brothers and sisters, or their father, or their mother, who eventually died in prison of an undiagnosed ectopic pregnancy, a pregnancy which apparently even she did not know about.

It is too painful to think of the lives those children bear — too maddening to think how such things are possible. It is hard to imagine that any woman, whatever her problem, has no moment of clarity or remorse when she says, "Enough is enough. How many children must I destroy before I submit to sterilization?" What self-absorption, what utter disregard for children, what madness accounts for inflicting such pain on little children? And what kind of society allows this to happen repeatedly on some misguided notion of individual "rights," whether from the right or the left, *rights assumed not to apply to children?*

In those cases where no decision occurred but pregnancy results, the needs of the child-to-be must be part of the deliberation about whether to bring the pregnancy to term or whether to keep the child. Anything less is unacceptable and efforts to suppress the work of the organization most ready and able to help, Planned Parenthood, are unconscionable.

The central question women (and men) must ask when considering whether to have a child is: Would that child wish to be born into this set of circumstances. But the child-to-be cannot speak for itself, and hence, the common phrase, "She/he did not ask to be born."

Strangely, it is criminal to put a child in harm's way, but to give birth to a child in circumstances where harm faces the child at every turn is not a crime. Everywhere the presumed right of adults to propagate at will takes precedence over the inalienable right of every child to a decent life with minimal standards for growing and thriving, physically, intellectually and morally. That bears *serious* rethinking.

CHAPTER 7. TRASHING OUR WORLD

The Environmental and Human Impact of Having Children

Ga Ga Over Babies

Her beaming face positively glowed on the page and one could almost see the words spilling from her lips. Was she ready to have more babies, the interviewer asked the woman who already had two children? "Not right away," actress Gwyneth Paltrow answered demurely. But she added, "I have a dream version where I think, maybe in four years I'll have two in a row really quickly again — how fabulous to have a whole bunch of them!"[143]

A whole bunch of them . . .

Choosing Human Extinction

At one time, reproduction prevented the annihilation of the human species. Now reproduction threatens the very existence of the human species.

The world's population stands at an astounding 7 billion plus people.[144] Every year, approximately 131.4 million babies enter the world as life-spans of those already here grow increasingly longer. If this rate of growth continues, by the year 2050 our planet will hold 9.3 billion people.[145] If that sounds too far distant to take seriously, consider that many of us, and certainly our children and grandchildren, will live to see this — and experience all of its dire consequences. It will only take another 60 years for the world's population to double, propelling our planet ever more quickly toward catastrophe.

For decades the scientific community has raised the alarm, each time with growing urgency. *The Intergovernmental Panel on Climate Change Report*, written by more than 800 climate researchers and vetted by 2,500 scientists from 180 countries, warned that "warming of the climate system is unequivocal." They alerted us in the strongest terms that there is, at the very least, a 90% likelihood that releases of greenhouse gases caused by burning fossil fuels is resulting in more heat waves, longer and more severe droughts, more serious flooding, more turbulent storms, and other disasters — far worse, they said, than earlier studies.[146] Indeed, the hurricanes, tsunamis, flooding, super storms, droughts, forest fires, unusual heat waves, and the like, of recent years seem to bear out these alarming forecasts.

Humans depend completely on earth's geochemical and biological systems. We have been disrupting these systems and rendering countless species extinct for a long time by acidifying the oceans, destroying our tropical rainforests and changing the composition of our atmosphere. As ecologist Paul Ehrlich put it so well, "In pushing other species to extinction, humanity is busy sawing off the limb on which it perches."[147]

Despite the overwhelming scientific evidence of environmental degradation by human beings, a veritable industry exists in denying the facts. Underwritten by the likes of Exxon Mobil, with its vested interest in fossil fuels, and other corporate spoilers, as well as bought and paid for politicians, the naysayers plug on with their dangerous rhetoric.[148]

But being in denial doesn't change the facts. An exploding population increasingly finds itself squeezed between rising sea waters and expanding deserts. As we burn more and more fossil fuels, carbon dioxide emissions clog our atmosphere while ongoing deforestation reduces the number of trees able to absorb that carbon. The resulting global warming and destructive climate changes are shrinking arable land, dropping groundwater levels, and melting polar ice caps (Arctic sea ice covers only half the area it did just thirty years ago). All this intensifies the existing crisis in world hunger.

Most ominous, in roughly 100 years the United States coast line (and those of countries around the world) will be dramatically altered by flooding and storm surges caused by rapidly melting glaciers and disappearing ice sheets as the ocean rises about one meter or 39 inches.[149] Projections are that coastal cities will lose 10%–20% or more of their land (think New York City, Miami, Boston . . .). We are talking about a catastrophic impact on cities large and small, vital farmlands, recreational areas and infrastructure, as well as the displacement of large numbers of our population. New Orleans' experience with hurricane Katrina, the Northeast's clash with super storm Sandy, and the Philippines' brutal encounter with typhoon Haivan are previews of what's coming.

But we need not wait 100 years. Already we find ourselves squeezed by the growth of high density population centers, suburban sprawl, unsafe amounts of methane released by cattle herds, toxic agricultural run offs, dangerous levels of air and water pollution, and a looming shortage of fresh drinking water in many parts of the country. At least 36 states will soon face local, regional or statewide water shortages according to government projections.[150] Over-fishing, habitat destruction, the introduction of invasive species, and contamination increasingly result in dwindling or toxic fish in our oceans and lakes.

Put simply, our excessive consumption is no longer balanced by the earth's capacity to regenerate and take in our wastes. "Sustainability requires living with the regenerative capacity of the biosphere."[151] This requires a balance between human demands on the environment and the area needed for producing food, providing other human needs and absorbing human wastes. Scientists have calculated how much land is required for meeting the human demand for food, animal pastures, fishing, timber, infrastructure, and absorbing carbon dioxide that results from using fossil fuels. *Not since the 1980s has humanity's use of natural resources matched actual global supply.*[152] *The world has long since passed sustainability.*

What does this mean in practical terms? It means we are slowly breeding ourselves into extinction, along with the animal and plant species around us, many of which have already disappeared.

Meanwhile, roughly 1 billion people around the world suffer from chronic hunger. That's equivalent to more than the combined populations of the United States, Canada and the European Union — a lot of starving people.[153]

Of these hungry people, well over 9 million die each year from hunger related causes,[154] 6.5 million of them children.[155] We all need to try picturing the agonizing, slow, wasting death of starvation and multiply that picture by millions to begin appreciating this horrible scenario. Of course, the problem goes far beyond regional food shortages. Half of the world's population cannot afford to buy food and has little or no access to medicine, health care, electricity, and safe drinking water. The other half wastes food, water, and other resources.

It's Not Just Their Problem

Wealthy nations cannot remain smug about their plenty, believing this problem exists only for developing countries. Wars often flow from conflicts related to scare resources, like oil, and shrinking land available to growing populations. Millions of people unable to sustain themselves in their native countries migrate to wealthier nations, bringing a host of problems with them — lower wages, third world diseases, a huge strain on social services, education and health care, increases in urban population densities, a lower standard of living for everyone, a drain on already scare resources like water, and much more.

The United States is a case in point with the fastest population growth among developed countries, fueled by an additional 1.3 million legal immigrants[156] and up to 1.5 million illegal immigrants each year.[157] This is in addition to roughly four million births annually.[158] America's current population is over 315 million and represents the third fastest growing country in the world.[159]

Here's the wake-up call. We have known for some time that the maximum population for a *sustainable* economy in the United States is 200 million. Given the current numbers, to achieve sustainability America would have to reduce its population by at least one third.[160] Very simply, our current population growth is unsustainable.

Yet few in the environmental movement, few politicians, and few in the population at large, talk openly anymore about *the root cause of this impending environmental crisis — overpopulation —* with its disastrous consequences. It's far easier to talk about more fuel efficient cars, energy efficient light bulbs, reusable grocery bags, recycling, and the like. All of which are important. But these efforts will not save the planet if we continue to reproduce at current levels. If we drastically cut carbon emissions, but the population using fossil fuels continues to swell, we are no better off. Every additional one million people requires enormous amounts of food, fuel, and other resources to sustain life.

Ignore it or not, the source of the looming ecological and human calamity is overpopulation, and it is not being addressed. Perhaps politicians and environmentalists fear alienating those centered on the family and so-called "family values" who have come to hold so much power — members of evangelical and Catholic churches who oppose contraception and confuse human folly with "God's will."

Others, perhaps, have unbounded faith that science and technology can endlessly save us from ourselves. It cannot. Two decades ago the National Science Academies of 58 countries signed a joint statement warning all of us that science cannot forever solve problems caused by overpopulation.

Many continue to believe overpopulation is a problem only for developing countries with their high birth rates. In fact, population increases in the United States are every bit as dangerous for the world as unchecked population growth in third world nations. Americans consume a far greater proportion of the world's resources. For example, Americans use three times the amount of water per capita than the world average, even as the supply of fresh drinking water has declined dramatically.

Despite being only 5% of the world's population, the United States devours 25% of the world's energy. Nonetheless, Americans are not downsizing their homes, but building bigger homes, despite the utter waste of natural resources, energy, and land this requires. Every year farmland disappears into ever-expanding suburbia. Freshwater supplies shrink as population demands increase. Our inordinate appetite for meat means ever more cropland must be devoted to grains that feed animals and that the methane gas emitted by these animals contributes heavily to global warming. Our thirst for diminishing energy supplies has resulted in corn crops, once used to feed much of the world, increasingly diverted to ethanol production (which itself requires fossil fuels to generate). As we consume and waste so much and use the planet's resources at will, we do so off the backs of the world's poor and hungry.

The list of the United States' disproportionate use of the earth's bounty is so long that if everyone in the world consumed resources at our rate, the planet could only support 1.8 billion people, far less than the 7 billion of us.[161] Yet as more and more developing countries raise their standard of living by even a small amount and begin to use more resources, the crisis grows exponentially.

Having too many babies is *not* just a problem for developing countries. Having babies in the United States and other developed countries matters greatly as well.

A Most Unpleasant Question

Since the planet provides each of us everything necessary for life itself, what are our obligations to that planet? Or put the question differently. Is it ethical merely to take endlessly from the planet and give nothing back? We each need to ask some hard questions.

Do I have the right to act in a way that unnecessarily wastes or destroys any part of the planet and its resources, whether by intent, by carelessness, or by willful ignorance?

Since I share this planet with other human beings, what are our reciprocal rights and obligations toward each other?

Finally, if we care anything about ourselves, our progeny, our planet with its life-sustaining plant and animal species, then we must ask that most unpleasant of all questions: Do I have an absolute right to reproduce at will?

Dear reader, answer these questions for yourself as you see fit. For myself, the answers are as follows.

I found myself alive and helpless on this planet as a result of the activity of my parents and the planet that sustained their lives. Therefore, both parents, and by extension the planet, owed me as a child the necessities of life. The most minimal of these include food and water for nourishment, air to breathe, and shelter. On entering the world, I had a right to these things, as does any child. (Leave aside the elements of love and care already discussed.)

Because the planet enables me to live, because I continually take from its bounty (and must if I am to survive), I owe it something, if for no reason other than enlightened self interest. (I leave it for others to make the religious argument for stewardship of God's earth.) My symbiotic relationship with the planet entails reciprocity, a give and take by both parties. Reciprocity is the necessary condition for two things: my survival and the planet's ability to keep giving to me and my progeny. It takes no great leap of reason to understand this last point. On the basis of enlightened self-interest, I am obliged to act in such a way that I preserve and protect the planet's ability to keep giving.

It seems patently self-evident that I do *not* have the right to act in a way that *unnecessarily* wastes or destroys any part of the planet and its resources, whether by intent, by carelessness, or by willful ignorance. If, for example, I build a house for myself that goes far beyond my necessity for shelter and a reasonably happy life — say, a 6,000 square feet home when a 2,000 square feet house would more than suffice — I am unnecessarily wasting timber and contributing to deforestation, not to mention the amount of land required by the larger home, the habitat destruction and sprawl, and the huge amount of electricity and other fuel required, much of it produced by fossil fuels. These excesses matter, of course, because I *am not alone.*

Which raises the point of how we as humans sharing the planet are obliged to act toward each other. Just as I entered the world with certain basic rights, so too does everyone. Whether I was fortunate enough through no action on my part to be born into affluence rather than poverty is beside the point. Fortuna is random and confers on me no special *rights*, although she may give me special *privileges*.

Therefore I cannot act in such a way that presumes a special status with special rights vis-à-vis others and the planet. I have the same right to use the earth's bounty as others — no more, no less — and I have the same duty to preserve and protect the environment as everyone — no more, no less. Part of this duty entails consideration of the needs of others when taking from the earth. How, for example, do I justify willfully wasting food in such a way as to limit the food available to others? Or how do I justify routinely burning fossil fuels unnecessarily when that contributes to global warming?

The great conservationist Theodore Roosevelt affirmed a simple principle, "I recognize the right and duty of this generation to develop and use the natural resources of our land; but I do not recognize the right to waste them, or to rob, by wasteful use, the generations that come after us."[162] He also said, "The conservation of natural resources is the fundamental problem. Unless we solve that problem it will avail us little to solve all others."[163]

This consideration of the needs of others — all of us together — applies not just to my ongoing use of earth's resources. It also pertains to the very question of how I am affecting the planet by adding to the world's population. (It's a connection, incidentally, that even Teddy Roosevelt failed to make when he took to task a clergyman of his day who urged limiting family size to two children).[164]

What, then, of that most unpleasant of all questions: Do I have an absolute right to reproduce at will? On the basis of enlightened self-interest which extends to my progeny, my neighbors and my planet with its life-sustaining resources, the answer is no. I have no special standing that would justify reproducing as many babies as I "want." If I were to act willfully in this way, I would set in motion a chain reaction with my children likely having children, and their children's children likely having children, and their children's children likely having children, and . . . We never just "bring one child into the world."

Certainly there was a time when there were so few of us on earth that it did not matter. But those days have long since past, as have the days when we lacked authoritative information about what is happening to our environment and the days when we lacked effective means, contraceptives, to limit family size. In the twenty-first century, reproduction at will can only be *explained* (not justified) by ignorance, extreme self-absorption, lack of means to control conception, female subordination, or religious beliefs.

By any rational measure, I am obliged to give reproduction thoughtful, careful, loving consideration, not just from a personal perspective (how children will fit my life and circumstances), but from a global perspective (how this will impact the environment, my fellow human beings and future generations). In short, I am obliged to act responsibly in conceiving life.

Consider Adopting

Do we really need to endlessly replicate ourselves when our crowded planet holds so many children desperate for a home? Is there a risk in adopting? Of course. But so are there risks in having our own children.

Nothing in life is without risk. The question comes down to the most serious and potentially devastating risk. By any measure, overpopulation and its consequence, environmental degradation and destruction, looms at the top of the list.

The "Urge" to Reproduce

Throughout human history, since time immemorial, we have been taught that a woman's primary value — many would say her *only* value — is as wife and mother. If she is not a wife and mother, we throw slurs at her: old maid and spinster (no comparable terms exist for men). And even if she marries, she is "barren" or "unfulfilled" if she fails to produce children (unlike men who are without children). I have heard men refer to women without children as "brittle."

It is the rare person who breaks free of this ideological stranglehold regarding woman's "purpose" in life. Even one as enlightened as Theodore Roosevelt fell prey, *despite* his strong advocacy of women's rights — the right to vote, the right to hold and use property, the right to enter any profession she desired, the right to equal pay.[165] He affirmed:

> "There are certain old truths which will be true as long as the world endures, and which no amount of progress can alter . . . One of these truths is that . . . the primary duty of the woman is to be the helpmate, the housewife and mother. The woman who deliberately forgoes these blessings . . . such a creature merits contempt as hearty as any visited upon the soldier who

runs away in battle. . . The existence of women of this type forms one of the most unpleasant and unwholesome features of modern life."[166]

Throughout history women have taken the bait and overwhelmingly continue to buy into this mandate by accepting as immutable truth that having babies is *the* overarching mission in their lives.

But, some will object, the urge to reproduce is natural, a built-in instinct for both men and women. Let me suggest, as many have before me, that the *natural* "urge" being described is really the urge to have sex, not to reproduce. Infants are typically by-products of sex in the same way that trees are the by-product of a squirrel's urge to store acorns against hunger. When the squirrel "naturally" buries the acorn, a tree may result.[167] When couples have sex, a baby may result. Hence the astounding number of "unplanned" pregnancies.

Reproduction has been inculcated into every woman as the necessary feature of her life by male-dominated culture and religion, both of which have a vested interest in her reproducing. The indoctrination is so intense from her earliest childhood with its plethora of dolls, that the "urge" to have a baby is seen as a biological mandate. Sociologists, biologists, and psychologists, based on a large body of research, have debunked the idea of a *biological* maternal instinct. To the extent there is a maternal nurturing propensity, it likely is learned. If an innate instinct existed, why would culture and religion be at such pains to indoctrinate and pressure females to become mothers? How can we account for the huge number of neglectful and abusive mothers? We too easily confuse biological *possibility* with biological *necessity*.

But whatever the source of this "mandate" that every woman should bear children, be it learned or biological, the population explosion in recent times, with its destructive impact on the environment, our quality of life, and life itself, changes everything. It is a recipe for disaster over the coming decades. This impending calamity must be brought to the forefront of every woman's decision about whether to reproduce or not and about the number of children to have if she does.

It's Life

Life is full of possibilities and opportunities — if we don't shut them down. We create who we are by taking control, by acting deliberately and thoughtfully, by considering the consequences of our choices. Motherhood is the most serious choice of all and it has the most far-reaching consequences — for women, their partners, their children, their families, their communities, the earth itself. It deserves to be more than an unthinking, knee-jerk response to centuries of cultural conditioning.

AUTHOR'S NOTE

The many personal stories recounted here represent decades of interactions with women, both professional and personal. In order to protect their privacy, the names used are all fictitious, with the exception, of course, of the names of public figures who are quoted and cited. In the stories, circumstantial details not relevant to the points being made (like place, time, job, and the like) have also been changed to protect privacy. In some instances, a story may represent multiple women who lived through a similar experience, in which case the story is a composite picture of all those women. In every instance, my concern has been to protect privacy.

ENDNOTES

1 Jeannine O. Howitz, "Reflections of a Feminist Mom," *On the Issues*, Fall, 1993, pp. 15-16.

2 Naomi Wolf, *Misconceptions: Truth, Lies and the Unexpected on the Journey to Motherhood* (New York: Anchor, 2003), pp. 1-10.

3 Louis Genevie and Eva Margolies, *The Motherhood Report: How Women Feel About Being Mothers* (New York: Macmillan, 1987), p. 15.

4 "My Life Is a Waking Nightmare," www.slate.com , Feb. 6, 2014.

5 "Parental Pity Party," New York Times, Op-Ed, Feb. 6, 2014.

6 Genevie and Margolies, p. 4.

7 Rosie Jackson, *Mothers Who Leave: Behind the Myth of Women Without Their Children* (London: Harper Collins, 1994), p. 247.

8 Genevie and Margolies, p. 16.

9 Naomi Wolf, *Misconceptions*, Ann Crittenden, *The Price of Motherhood*, Jessica Mitford, *The American Way of Birth*.

10 Elizabeth Badinter, "The Tyranny of Breast-Feeding: New Mothers vs. LaLeche League," Harper's, March, 2012, pp. 39-44.

11 Wolf, p. 268.

12 Ibid., p. 131.

13 Ibid., p. 268.

14 Judith Warner, *Perfect Madness: Motherhood in the Age of Anxiety* (New York: Riverhead, 2006), p. xiv.

15 Kathleen Deveny, "Yummy vs. Slummy," *Newsweek*, August 13, 2007, p. 44.

16 Ibid., p. 133. For a review of the studies, see pp. 298-299.

17 Lauren Sandler, "The American Nightmare," *Psychology Today*, March/April, 2011, p. 74.

18 John Rosemond, Syndicated column, "Parents and Kids," *Syracuse Post Standard*, May 31, 1996.

19 Ibid.

20 Ranae J. Evenson and Robin W. Simon, "Clarifying the Relationship Between Parenthood and Depression," *Journal of Health and Social Behavior*, December, 2005, pp. 341-358.

21 AARP Fact Sheet, October, 2006.

22 "Grandparents as Parents," The National Committee to Preserve Social Security and Medicare, November, 2002.

23 Carin Rubenstein, "The Baby Bomb," *New York Times Good Health Magazine*, October 8, 1989, pp. 34-40, looks at a number of studies which reveal the uneven burden women bear. See also Arlie Hochschild and Anne Machung, *The Second Shift* (New York: Penguin, 2012).

24 Jody Heymann, *The Widening Gap: Why American Families are in Jeopardy and What Can Be Done About It* (New York: Basic Books, 2000), p. 149.

25 Genevie and Margolis, pp. 335-336.

26 Elizabeth Aura McClintock, Study presented to the American Sociological Association meeting, August 13, 2013, using data from 1981 to 2009. See also Hochschild and Machung, based on an eight year study of working couples.

27 University of Michigan study, in Andrew Hacker, *Mismatch: The Growing Gulf Between Men and Women* (New York: Scribner, 2003), p. 56.

28 Hochschild and Machung, p. 252.

29 Kathleen Deveny, "We're Not in the Mood," *Newsweek*, June 30, 2003, pp. 40.

30 Wolf, pp. 225-273.

31 Carin Rubenstein, "The Baby Bomb," *New York Times Good Health Magazine*, October 8, 1989, pp. 34-40.

32 Ibid.

33 Genevie and Margolis, p. 338.

34 Work and Family Institute/Louis Harris Study.

35 Howitz, p. 15.

36 Mary Kay Blakely, "An Outlaw Mom Tells All," *MS.*, January/February, 1995, p. 41.

37 Family Caregiver Alliance. See Factsheets at www.caregiver.org.

38 Andrea Gabor, "Married, With Househusband," *Working Woman*, Novem-

ber, 1995, p. 96.

39 Harriet Braiker, *The Type E Woman* (Australia: Harper Collins, 1987).

40 Gallup Survey, December, 1988.

41 Roberta Israeloff, "Steady As She Goes: Balancing Work, Family and Leisure," *Working Woman*, July, 1991.

42 *Ladies Home Journal* survey, "What Moms Love," November 1, 2000, p. 154.

43 Gwen Sublette, "Balancing Act," *Entrepreneurial Woman*, Summer, 1993.

44 TV Replay, The Ricki Lake Show, AOL HUFFPOST Entertainment, March 1, 2013.

45 Norval Glenn and Sara McLanahan, "Children and Marital Happiness," *Journal of Marriage and Family*, 44, 1, February, 1982, pp. 63-72. The authors studied six national surveys of various sub-populations in the U.S. between 1973-1978 and found that on average, children adversely affect marital quality.

L. White, A. Booth and J. Edwards, "Children and Marital Happiness: Why the Negative Correlation," *Journal of Family Issues*, 7, 1986, pp. 131-147.

J. Belsky, "Children and Marriage" in *The Psychology of Marriage* edited by F. D. Fincham and T. N. Bradbury, (New York: Guilford, 1990), pp. 172-200.

Tim B. Heaton, "Marital Stability Throughout the Child-rearing Years" *Demography* 27 (1990), pp. 55-63.

Linda Waite and Lee A. Lillard, "Children and Marital Disruption" *American Journal of Sociology* 96 (1991), pp. 930-953.

More recently, data from 148 studies over 5 decades were analyzed and confirmed this finding: Jean M. Twenge, W. Campbell and Craig Foster, "Parenthood and Marital Satisfaction: A Meta-Analytical review," *Journal of Marriage and Family*, August, 2003, pp. 574-583.

46 Twenge, et. al., p. 580.

47 Genevie and Margolies, p.16.

48 Carin Rubenstein, p. 34. See also Susan Herrick with Dr. Kathy Richie, "Marital Interaction: What Are Its Predicators?" *Indiana University Undergraduate Journal*, Vol. 1, 1998, www.iusb.edu/ugr-journal/static/1993/paper7.php; and Ellen Walker, "Fact or Fiction: Childfree Couples Are Happier Than Couples With Kids," *Psychology Today*, March 31, 2011, http://www.psychologytoday.com/blog/complete-without-kids/201103/fact-or-fiction-childfree-couples-are-happier-couples-kids.

49 Professor David Popenoe, "The National Marriage Project," From 1997 to 2002, Rutgers University.

50 Twenge, et. al., pp. 579, 580.

51 American Psychological Association and the National Institute of Mental Health. Also see Saju Joy, M.D., "Post Partum Depression," Medscape.com, March 6, 2012, http://reference.Medscape.com/article/271662-overview.

52 H. Feldman, "Development of the Husband-Wife Relationship," Unpublished manuscript, Cornell University, 1965. See also, Karen Polonko, John Scanzoni and Jay Teachman, "Childlessness and Marital Satisfaction," *Journal of Family Issues*, December, 1982, pp. 545-573.

53 Twenge, et. al., pp. 579.

54 Maggie Scarf, *Intimate Partners: Patterns in Love And Marriage* (New York: Ballantine, 2008), p. 169.

55 Tracy Hotchner, *Childbirth and Marriage* (New York: Avon, 1989), p. 139.

56 Sheila Kitzinger, *Women As Mothers* (New York: Random House, 1979), p.174.

57 Family Life Survey, *Parents*, November, 1996, pp. 128-130.

58 Ibid.

59 Syracuse *Post Standard*, October 22, 1996, p. C2.

60 Hotchner, p. 33.

61 E. E. LeMasters, "Parenthood as Crisis" in *Marriage and Family Living*, 19, 1957, pp. 352-355.

62 John M. Guttman and Alyson F. Shapiro, "Bringing Baby Home" (An Abstract), Seattle, WA: Relationship Research Institute, p. 2.

For a more complete analysis see Cowan, C. P. and P. A. Cowans, *When Partners Become Parents*, (New York: Basic Books, 2000).

63 Genevie and Margolies, p. 126. See also Twenge, et. al., pp. 574-583.

64 Hotchner, p.58.

65 Genevie and Margolies, p. 153.

66 Ibid., p. 152.

67 National institute of Mental Health; National Alliance of Mental Illness.

68 Centers for Disease Control and Prevention, 2012. 16% of high school students seriously consider suicide and 8% attempt suicide.

69 Genevie and Margolies pp. 180,184.

70 Susan Brown and I-Fen Lin, "The Gray Divorce Revolution," research report, National Center for Family and Marriage Research, 2010.

71 Ibid.

72 Jane Glenn Haas, syndicated columnist, "After 50, Women May Scorn Remarrying," *Syracuse Post Standard*, August 12, 2007, p. I-3.

73 Ibid.

74 Arizona State University study, 1997, cited by Dr. Dan Neuharth in "To Be, or Not To Be, a Parent," www.controllingparents.com/choosing-toparent.htm.

75 Judith Warner, *Perfect Madness*, p. 289.

76 For an extensive discussion see Diane E. Eyer, *Mother-Infant Bonding: A Scientific Fiction* (New Haven: Yale University. 1993).

77 U.S. Census Bureau.

78 Suzanne Bianchi, Lekha Subaiya and Joan R. Kahn, "The Gender Gap in the Economic Well-Being of Non-resident Fathers and Custodial Mothers," *Demography*, 36, 2, 1999, pp. 195-203. They found that the economic well-being of custodial mothers dropped by 36% and the well-being of non-resident fathers rose by 28%.

See also Jennifer L. Gerson, Howard Iams, and Gayle Reznik, "Work Patterns and Marital Status Change," *Family and Economic Issues*, Spring, 1990, pp. 7-21.

79 Georgia Binstock and Arland Thornton, "Separations, Reconciliations, and Living Apart in Cohabiting and Marital Unions," *Journal of Marriage and Family*, May, 2003, pp. 432-443. See also Matthew D. Bramlett and William D. Mosher, "Cohabitation, Marriage, Divorce, and Remarriage," Center for Disease Control, July 24, 2002, pp. 37-41.

80 U.S. Census Bureau, 2001.

81 Joyce Jacobsen, Rhodes College, and Laurence Levin, Santa Clara University, in their 1992 in-depth, longitudinal study, found that women who left the work force, even for just six months, were still making less money than their peers 20 years later. Similarly, a study by Professor Schneer of Rider University and Professor Reitman at Pace University found that female M.B.A.s who left the workforce for a relatively brief period — 8.8 months on average — earned 17% less in 1993 than women who did not leave the workforce.

82 U.S. Census Bureau, as analyzed in *Legal Momentum*, "Women's Poverty in the United States, 2011," p. 1.

83 "A Profile of Older Americans, 2011," United States Department of Health and Human Services, p. 3.

84 For example, Professor Schneer of Rider University and Professor Reitman at Pace University, found that female M.B.A.s who left the workforce for a relatively brief period — 8.8 months on average — did not advance as much as women who stayed in the workforce. Of the female M.B.A.s they studied, 60% of those who had not left the workforce had reached upper middle management or higher while only 44% of the M.B.A.s who left temporarily to have children reached those same levels.

85 Paulette Light, "Why 43% of Women With Children Leave Their Jobs,

and How to Get Them Back," *The Atlantic*, April 19, 2013, http://www.theatlantic.com/sexes/archive/2013/04/why-43-of-women-with-children-leave-their-jobs-and-how-to-get-them-back/275134/

86 Pew Center for Worklife Law, 2005. (The results exceed 100% because some did more than one of these things.)

87 The list of studies on the price women will pay for having babies is long and consistent. To mention a couple: One longitudinal study that tracked college educated women now in their mid-30s to late 40s (their demographic features closely match those of comparable women in the overall U.S. population) found that only one out of six college educated women had both a career and children by the time they reached middle age, Harvard economist Claudia Goldin, using data from the National Longitudinal Survey, 1991 update of the "Young Women" study, as reported in *Working Woman*, 1995.

Deborah Swiss and Judith Walker, *Women and the Work/Family Dilemma*, (Hoboken: Wiley, 1994) studied senior professional women between the ages of 32 and 57, all graduates of Harvard's professional schools. Virtually all of the 594 mothers in the group said they had encountered some discrimination from the point when they announced their pregnancy until well past returning to work. As a consequence, moms holding the MBA had a 25% drop-out rate, lawyers an 11% drop-out rate, and doctors a 4% drop-out rate.

88 Pamela Kruger, "Superwoman's Daughters," in *Working Woman*, May, 1994, p. 61.

89 Louise Story, "Many Women at Elite Colleges Set Career Path to Motherhood," *New York Times*, Sept. 20, 2005, pp. 1, 18.

90 Dunhill Personnel System, Woodbury, NY, 1994. For an extensive discussion, see also Dorothy C. Holland and Margaret A. Eisenhart, *Educated in Romance* (Chicago: University of Chicago Press, 1990).

91 Kruger, p.61.

92 Ibid.

93 Lorena Blas, "The Bumpy Ride is Over for Ryder," *USA TODAY*, July, 17, 2007, p. D3.

94 U.S. Census Bureau, June, 2004.

95 See Madelyn Cain, *The Childless Revolution* (New York: DeCapo, 2001), for a discussion of these issues.

96 HuffPost Live, Feb. 17, 2014.

97 McGill Institute for Health and Social Policy and the Project on Global Working Families, 2006. Although no data exists for a handful of countries, the United States is in the company of Swaziland, Liberia, Papua New Guinea, and Australia in providing some of the world's

weakest leave benefits.

For a summary of an interesting comparative study conducted by London economist Claire Kilpatrick and presented in a paper at the European University, see *Working Woman* magazine, September, 1995, p. 12. Kilpatrick compares France, with many support services in place for working mothers and England, with far fewer. She quantifies the benefits to mothers and fathers, not to mention families, when social support services are in place.

98 Ann Landers syndicated column, 1975.

99 "60 Minutes," CBS, August 4, 2007.

100 Judith Warner, "Mommy Madness," *Newsweek*, Feb. 21, 2006, p. 44.

101 For an extended study of women who leave their children, see Rosie Jackson, *Mothers Who Leave*.

102 Nora Okja Keller, "You'll Get Used To It," in *Mothers Who Think* edited by Camille Peri and Kate Moses (New York: Washington Square Press, 1999), p. 114.

103 Ibid., pp. 116-118.

104 Elinor Gadon, *The Once and Future Goddess* (New York: Harper Collins, 1989). p. 289.

105 Susan Patton, *Marry Smart* (New York: Gallery Books, 2014).

106 Sylvia Ann Hewlett, *Creating a Life: Professional Women and the Quest for Children* (New York: Hyperion, 2002).

107 Warner, *Perfect Madness*, p. 61. Based on Shel Silverstein's children's book, *The Giving Tree*.

108 Cathleen Collins Lee, "Another Baby? Maybe . . . Not," *Parents*, October, 1993, p. 46.

109 Susan S. Lang, *Women Without Children* (Avon, MA: Adams Media, 1996), p. 205.

110 U.S. Department of Agriculture, 2011.

111 U.S. Dept. of Education, 2012.

112 M. P. Dunleavey, "Cost of Being a Stay-at-Home Mom," originally published on *Money Central* at MSN.com, www.newparent.com/mom/the-cost-of-being-a-stay-at-home-mom.

113 The Working Poor Families Project, 2012.

114 The National Center for Women and Retirement Research, cited in "Suddenly Single," *Working Woman*, September, 1996, p. 32.

115 *Syracuse Post Standard*, Nov. 23, 2008, pp. 1, 14.

116 *Syracuse Post Standard*, Nov. 23, 2008. p. 4.

117 Sharon E. Epperson and Elaine Rivera, "Abandoned To Her Fate," *Time*

Magazine cover story, December 11, 1995, pp. 32-36.

118 "Child Maltreatment: Facts at the Glance," Center for Disease Control and Prevention, 2012.

119 U.S. Government Accountability Office, 2011.

120 ChildHelp.org.

121 Grant, B. "Estimates of U.S. Children Exposed to Alcohol Abuse and Dependence in the Family,"*American Journal of Public Health*, Jan. 2000, pp. 90, 112.

122 L. Dickinson, et. al., "Health Related Quality of Life and Symptoms Profiles of Female Survivors of Sexual Abuse," *Arch Family Medicine*, 1999, 8, 35-43. See also David Finkelhor, et. al., "Victimization of Children and Youth: A Comprehensive National Survey," *Child Maltreatment*, February 1, 2005, p. 6.

123 Cindy Rodriguez, "Teen Left To Fend For Herself," Syracuse *Post Standard*, October 11, 1996, p. C1.

124 Ibid.

125 For an account of this case, see Joyce Johnson, *What Lisa Knew: The Truth and Lies of the Steinberg Case* (New York: Putnam, 1990).

126 Ibid.

127 "Understanding Intimate Partner Violence" (Fact Sheet), Center for Disease Control and Prevention, 2012.

128 Child Welfare Information Gateway, "Domestic Violence and the Child Welfare System" (Report), 2009, pp. 2-4.

129 "Child Maltreatment," U.S. Department of Health and Human Services, 2011.

130 "Child Maltreatment: Facts at a Glance," Center for Disease Control and Prevention, 2012.

131 ChildHelp, 2012, www.childhelp.org/pages/statistics.

132 Ibid.

133 "Long-Term Consequences of Child Abuse and Neglect," Child Welfare Information Gateway and United States Department of Health and Human Services, 2013.

134 Ibid.

135 Ibid.

136 National Vital Statistics Report, Center for Disease Control, 2012. See also www.childtrenddatabank.org.

137 "11 Facts About Teen Pregnancy," www.dosomething.org using data from the United States Center for Disease Control and Prevention, the Guttmacher Institute, and the National Campaign to Prevent Teen

and Unplanned Pregnancy.

138 "Facts on American Teens Sexual and Reproductive Health" (Fact Sheet), Guttmacher Institute, June, 2013.

139 Mark Mather, Ph.D., "U.S. Children in Single Mother Families," Population Reference Bureau, May, 2010, pp. 1-2.

140 Letter to Abigail Van Buren, 1996.

141 "Facts on Unintended Pregnancy in the Unites States" (Fact Sheet), Guttmacher Institute, October, 2012.

142 "Facts on American Teens Sexual and Reproductive Health" (Fact Sheet), Guttmacher Institute, June, 2013.

143 Catherine Hong, "Gwyneth Paltrow," W magazine, September, 2007, www.wmagazine.com/people/celebrities/2007/09/gwyneth_paltrow

144 U.S. Census Bureau. 2013.

145 Ibid.

146 2007 Report.

147 Sign in the Hall of Biodiversity, American Museum of Natural History, New York.

148 For a summary, see Sharon Begley, "The Truth About Denial," cover story in *Newsweek*, August 13, 2007, pp. 20-29.

149 University of Arizona Study based on data from the U.S. Geological Service, September, 2007, widely reported by the Associated Press.

150 "Water Supply in the U.S.," Environmental Protection Agency, www.epa.gov/watersense/pubs/supply.html.

151 Mathis Wackernagel, et. al., "Tracking the Ecological Overshoot of the Human Economy," *Proceedings of the National Academy of Sciences*, Vol. 99, No. 14, June 25, 2002, p. 9266.

152 Ibid., pp. 9266-9271.

153 United Nations World Food program and the World Bank, 2012.

154 World Health Organization, 2012.

155 UNICEF, 2006.

156 Census Bureau, 2006.

157 Pew Hispanic Data Estimates, 2006.

158 National Center for Health Statistics. Center for Disease Control and Prevention, 2004.

159 U.S. Census Bureau, January, 2013.

160 For an extensive discussion, see David Pimentel and Mario Giampietro, *Food, Land, Population and the U.S. Economy*, (San Francisco: Carrying Capacity Network, 1994).

161 United Nations, June, 2005.

162 "The New Nationalism" speech, Osawatomie, Kansas, August 31, 1910.

163 Address to the Deep Waterway Convention, Memphis, TN, October 4, 1907.

164 "On American Motherhood," a speech delivered to the National Congress of Mothers, Washington, D.C., March 13, 1905.

165 Theodore Roosevelt, *An Autobiography* (New York: Macmillan, 1913), pp. 49-51.

166 "On American Motherhood."

167 The analogy is not new to me. www.vhemt.org/biobreed.htm.

SELECTED BIBLIOGRAPHY

Belsky, J., "Children and Marriage" in *The Psychology of Marriage* edited by F. D. Fincham and T. N. Bradbury. New York: Guilford, 1990.

Bianchi, Suzanne, Lekha Subaiya and Joan R. Kahn, "The Gender Gap in the Economic Well-Being of Non-resident Fathers and Custodial Mother." *Demography*, 36, 2, 1999.

Blakely, Mary Kay, "An Outlaw Mom Tells All." *MS*. January/February, 1995.

Braiker, Harriet, *The Type E Woman*. Australia: Harper Collins, 1987.

Carter, Lucy S., et. al., "Domestic Violence and Children: Analysis and Recommendations." *Domestic Violence and Children*, Winter, 1999.

Cain, Madelyn, *The Childless Revolution*. New York: DeCapo Press, 2001.

Cowan, Carolyn P. and Philip A. Cowan, *When Partners Become Parents*. New York: Basic Books, 2000.

Crittenden, Ann, *The Price of Motherhood: Why the Most Important Job in the World is Still the Least Valued*. New York: Henry Holt, 2001.

DeFago, Nicki, *Childfree and Loving It*. London: Fusion, 2005.

Deveny, Kathleen, "We're Not in the Mood." *Newsweek*, June 30, 2003.

Deveny, Kathleen, "Yummy vs. Slummy." *Newsweek*, August 13, 2007.

Dickinson,L., et. Al., "Health Related Quality of Life and Symptoms Profiles of Female Survivors of Sexual Abuse." *Arch Family Medicine*, 1999, 8.

Douglas, Susan and Meredith Michaels, *The Mommy Myth: The Idealization of Motherhood and How It Has Undermined All Women*. New York: Free Press, 2005.

Epperson, Sharon and Elaine Rivera, "Abandoned To Her Fate." *Time Magazine* cover story, December 11, 1995.

Eyer, Diane E., *Mother-Infant Bonding: A Scientific Fiction.* New Haven: Yale University Press, 1993.

Gabor, Andrea, "Married, With Househusband." *Working Woman*, November, 1995.

Genevie, Louis and Eva Margolies, *The Motherhood Report: How Women Feel About Being Mothers.* New York: Macmillan, 1987.

Glenn, Norval and Sara McLanahan, "Children and Marital Happiness." *Journal of Marriage and Family*, February, 1982

"Grandparents as Parents" (Report). The National Committee to Preserve Social Security and Medicare, November, 2002.

Grant, B., "Estimates of U.S. Children Exposed to Alcohol Abuse and Dependence in the Family." *American Journal of Public Health*, January, 2000.

Hacker, Andrew, *Mismatch: The Growing Gulf Between Men and Women.* New York: Scribner, 2007.

Heaton, Tim B., "Marital Stability Throughout the Child-Rearing Years." *Demography* 27, 1990.

Herrick, Susan with Dr. Kathy Richie, "Marital Interaction: What Are Its Predicators?" *Indiana University Undergraduate Journal*, Vol. 1, 1998.

Hewlett, Sylvia Ann, *Creating a Life: Professional Women and the Quest for Children.* New York: Hyperion, 2002.

Heymann, Jody, *The Widening Gap: Why American Families are in Jeopardy and What Can Be Done About It.* New York: Basic Books, 2000.

Hochschild, Arlie and Anne Machung, *The Second Shift: Working Families and the Revolution at Home.* New York: Penguin, 2012.

Holland, Dorothy C. and Margaret A. Eisenhart, *Educated in Romance.* Chicago, University of Chicago Press, 1990.

Hotchner, Tracy, *Childbirth and Marriage.* New York: Avon, 1989.

Howitz, Jeannine O., "Reflections of a Feminist Mom." *On the Issues*, Fall, 1993.

Israeloff, Roberta, "Steady As She Goes: Balancing Work, Family and Leisure." *Working Woman*, July, 1991.

Jackson, Rosie, *Mothers Who Leave: Behind the Myth of Women Without Their Children.* Kitchener, Ont: Pandora, 1994.

Johnson, Joyce, *What Lisa Knew: The Truth and Lies of the Steinberg Case.* New York: Putnam, 1990.

Joy, Saju and David Chelmow, "Post Partum Depression." Medscape.com, March 6, 2012.

Keller, Nora Okja, "You'll Get Used To It" in *Mothers Who Think* edited by C. Peri and K. Moses. New York: Random House, 1999.

Kolbert, Elizabeth. *The Sixth Extinction: An Unnatural History.* New York: Henry Holt, 2014.

Kruger, Pamela, "Superwoman's Daughters." *Working Woman*, May, 1994.

Lang, Susan S., *Women Without Children: The Reasons, The Rewards, The Regrets.* Avon, MA: Adams Media, 1996.

Lee, Cathleen Collins, "Another Baby? Maybe . . . Not." *Parent's Magazine*, October, 1993.

LeMasters, E. E., "Parenthood as Crisis," *Marriage and Family Living*, vol. 19, 1957.

Maushart, Susan, *The Mask of Motherhood: How Becoming a Mother Changes Our Lives and Why We Never Talk About It.* New York: Penguin, 2000.

Peri, Camille and Kate Moses (editors), *Women Who Think.* New York: Washington Square Press, 2000.

Pimentel, David and Mario Giampietro, *Food, Land, Population and the U.S. Economy.* San Francisco: Carrying Capacity Network, 1994.

Polonko, Karen, John Scanzoni and Jay Teachman, "Childlessness and Marital Satisfaction." *Journal of Family Issues*, December, 1982.

Rich, Adrienne, Of Woman Born: Motherhood as Experience and Institution. New York: W. W. Norton, 1995.

Rubenstein, Carin, "The Baby Bomb." *New York Times Good Health Magazine*, October 8, 1989.

Scarf, Maggi, *Intimate Partners: Patterns in Love and Marriage.* New York: Ballantine, 2008.

Senior, Jennifer, *All Joy and No Fun: The Paradox of Modern Parenthood.* New York: Ecco, 2014.

Story, Louise, "Many Women at Elite Colleges Set Career Path to Motherhood." *New York Times*, Sept. 20, 2005.

Sublette, Gwen, "Balancing Act." *Entrepreneurial Woman*, Summer, 1993.

Swiss, Deborah and Judith Walker, *Women and the Work/Family Dilemma.* Hoboken: Wiley, 1994.

Twenge, Jean M., W. Keith Campbell, and Craig A. Foster, "Parenthood and Marital Satisfaction: A Meta-Analytical Review." *Journal of Marriage and Family*, August, 2003.

Wackernagel, Mathis, et. Al., "Tracking the Ecological Overshoot of the Human Economy." *Proceedings of the National Academy of Sciences*, June 25, 2002.

Waite, Linda and Lee A. Lillard, "Children and Marital Disruption." *Ameri-*

can *Journal of Sociology*, 96, 1991.

Walker, Ellen, "Fact or Fiction: Childfree Couples Are Happier Than Couples With Kids." *Psychology Today*, March 31, 2011.

Warner, Judith, "Mommy Madness." *Newsweek* cover story, Feb. 21, 2006.

Warner, Judith, *Perfect Madness: Motherhood in the Age of Anxiety*. New York: Riverhead, 2006.

White, L., A. Booth and J. Edwards, "Children and Marital Happiness: Why the Negative Correlation." *Journal of Family Issues*, 7, 1986.

Wolf, Naomi, *Misconceptions: Truth, Lies, and the Unexpected on the Journey to Motherhood*. New York: Anchor Books, 2003.

INDEX